U.S. MILITARY HISTORY

ACTIVITY WORKBOOK

U.S. Military

American Revolution / Civil War / WWI / WWII / GENERALS / SHIPS / PLANES / HEROES and ACES

INDEX

#	TITLE	Type of Puzzle	PAGE	ANS.	Related TRIVIA
1	ACES	Quiz	7	50	82
2	US Military General	Crossword	9	51	
3	BATTLESHIP	Quiz	11	52	84
4	FIGHTER PILOT	Observation	13	53	
5	NAME/RANK/SERIAL#	Quiz	14	54	85
6	US NAVY QUOTES	Cryptograms (4)	16	55	
7	JACKSON'S VALLEY CAMPAIGN	Dot to Dot	18	56	86
8	FAMOUS US BATTLES	Crossword	19	57	87
9	NORMANDY INVASION	Word Search	21	58	88
10	MILITARY - PRESIDENTS	Quiz	22	59	89
11	WWII AIR COMBAT	Observation	23	60	
12	HERACLITUS QUOTE	Cryptogram	24	61	
13	WAR IN AFGHANISTAN	Crossword	26	62	
14	PILOTS AND PLANES	Matching	28	63	90
15	WWII TANK KILLER	Observation	29	65	93
16	WWII HISTORY	Matching - Timeline	30	66	
17	PATTON QUOTES	Cryptograms (4)	31	67	
18	VIETNAM WAR	Crossword	33	67	
19	GUADALCANAL	Mazes (2)	35	69	95
20	WWI HISTORY	Matching - Timeline	36	70	

INDEX (II)

#	TITLE	Type of Puzzle	PAGE	ANS.	Related TRIVIA
21	MARINE WORDS	Word Search	37	71	97
22	FAMOUS GENERALS	Matching	38	72	98
23	QUOTES WWI & KOREA	Cryptograms (3)	39	73	
24	WWII WESTERN EUROPE	Fill-in-the Blanks	40	74	
25	WWII BATTLES	Word Search	41	75	
26	DOG FIGHT	Maze	42	76	
27	QUOTES by FAMOUS GENERALS	Cryptograms (3)	43	77	
28	NAVY – (FRIEND or FOE)	Observation	45	78	100
29	WWII – OCEAN WAR	Fill-in-the-Blanks	46	79	
30	REVOLUTION & CIVIL WAR QUOTES	Cryptograms (3)	47	80	

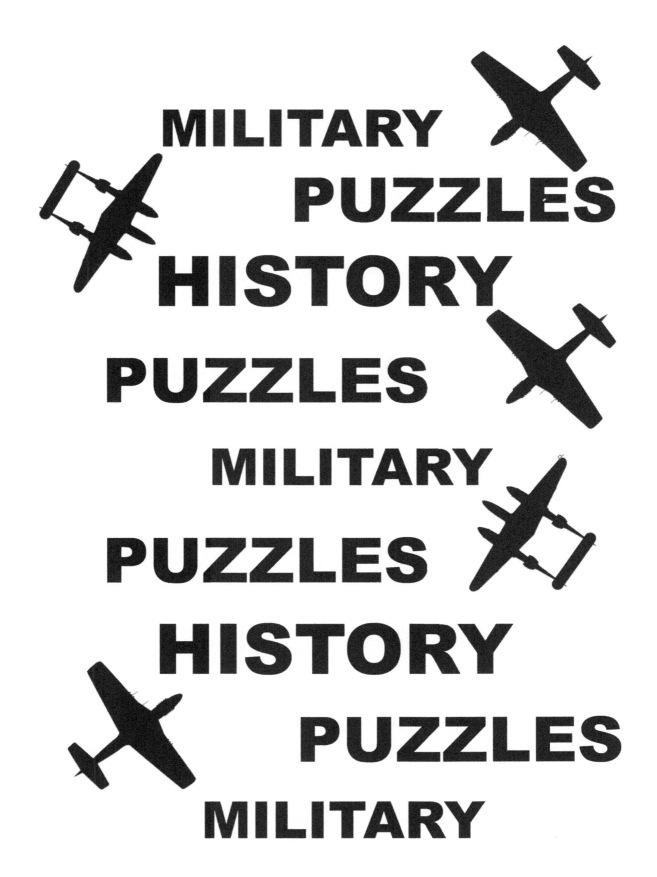

ACES

P U Z Z L E 1

Identify the aces, their nationality and if you are really good identify their # of victories (SEE HINTS ON THE NEXT PAGE)

Name	ACE Y/N	Nationality	Victories
Eric Hartmann			
Gregory Boyington			
Hosato Takei			
Hans Wind			
Aleksandr Pokryshkin			
Robert Stanford Tuck			
David Deihl			
Eino Luukkanen			
Eric Rudorffer			
Michael Faraday			
Shoichi Sugita			
Roger Sherman			
David Campbell			
Richard I. Bong			
Shigeo Fukumoto			
Yully Borisovich			
Jari Kurri			
Harold Scherer			
Spencer Chaplin			
Nevil Duke			
Ivan Koshedub			

P ACE HINTS
U
Z 1. NOT All people named were aces.
Z 2. Aces are from The USA, Britain, Russia, Germany
L   and Finland.
E 3. Victories were in one of (25-50), (50-100) (100 –
        200) and (Over 200)
1 4. Can you find the pilot with the most victories of all
        time?

ANSWER – 50 ---- TRIVIA - 82

PUZZLE 2

How much do you know about the US Military?

ANSWER – 51 ---- TRIVIA - --

PUZZLE #2 CLUES

Across

2. Invented GPS?
4. 11th hour, 11th day, 11th month – _____ day?
8. Commander in Chief of US Military?
9. Jeep?
11. Military version is 95% quieter than the traditional civilian version?
13. US Military is ALL _____?
16. Currently 1/2 of one percent of Americans are in the _____?
18. Department of Defense controls a land area the size of ____?
20. Each one is responsible for saving 150 to 1800 lives?
23. Clem joined the army at age___?
26. Dogs in the Military?
28. Prior to the Spanish-American war, US Military uniforms were___?
29. ____% of American families have a family member in the Active Service Military?
30. US has 2,150 deployed nuclear _____?
31. Number one killer of US Military troops?
32. 2nd Largest Employer in the US?
33. Sergeant John Lincoln Clem discharged at age___?
34. Women are restricted from ____ jobs in the military?

Down

1. Headquarters of the Department of Defense?
3. The month of the military child?
5. Uniform Code of Military Justice – qualifying punishment for 'Sleeping on the Post'?
6. The _____ War – 'Tomb of the Unknown Soldier' is Empty?
7. USMJ – Uniform ____ of Military Justice?
9. 1972 – 1995. Remote Viewing – Men Who Stare at _____?
10. Emergency water canteen in US Parachute Pack Survival Kits?
12. 400,000 US veterans rest at this site?
14. Secretary of Defense controls all military except___?
15. Male citizens must register with _____ Service?
17. 79,000 people ___ the military every year?
18. 1/2 of personnel in Afghanistan and Iraq are ____?
19. Austin Texas – approximate population of the US _____
21. 3rd US Infantry Regiment – The Old _____?
22. The US has formally declared war ____ times?
23. No. of US service men executed for crimes since 1961?
24. War with the most casualties?
25. US has the largest military budget in the world. ____ is second?
27. Largest Employer in the US?
28. Robot could carry 2000 lbs?
33. Use of Camouflage Uniforms began WW___?

PUZZLE 3

WWII BATTLESHIP – QUIZ

Objective 1: The first objective is to determine which ships are American Battleships and which are not.

Objective 2: The second objective of this QUIZ is to identify which ships listed are Battleships of other nations and which are not.

Objective 3: The third objective is (for those ships which are not Battleships), try to identify what kind of ship they are and what nation they belong to.

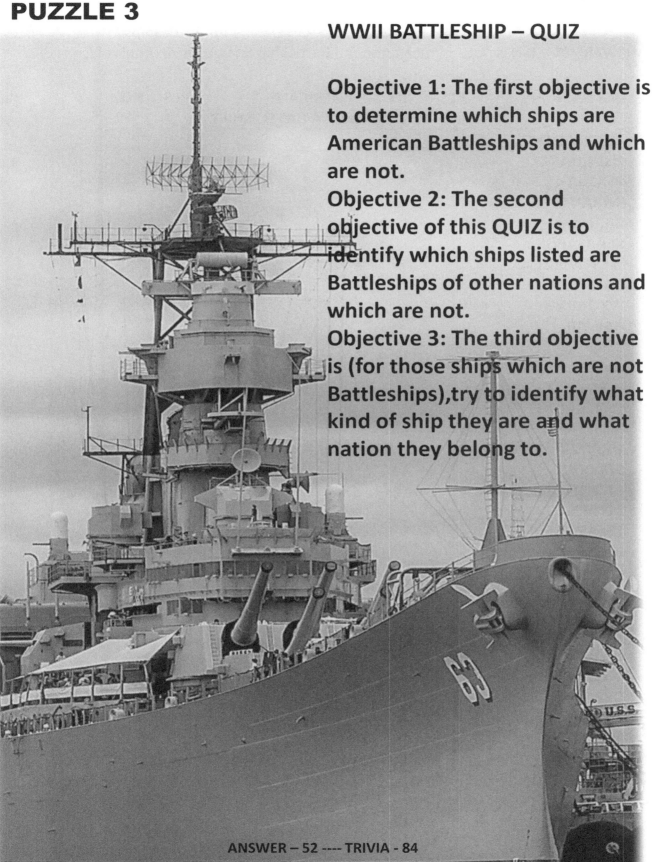

ANSWER – 52 ---- TRIVIA - 84

PUZZLE 3

WWII BATTLESHIPS – QUIZ – Do you know your Battleships
ANSWER Y/N – If it is not American or not a Battleship do you know what it is?

BATTLESHIP?	YES	NO	AMERICAN? NOT A BATTLESHIP?	YES	NO
COLORADO					
FLORIDA					
ALASKA					
INDIANA					
BARHAM					
KEARSARGE					
WEST VIRGINIA					
DALE					
WYOMING					
HAWAII					
OHIO					
AMERICA					
HOWE					
CENTURION					
MONTANA					
TIRPITZ					
ST LOUIS					
DAUNTLESS					
DENVER					
TEXAS					
IOWA					
PROVENCE					
CONGRESS					
DETROIT					
VIRGINIA					
UTAH					
INDEPENDENCE					
OREGON					
BENNINGTON					
REVENGE					
CONSTITUTION					
WASHINGTON					
FREEDOM					
NEW YORK					
CANBERRA					
ALABAMA					

PUZZLE 4

Fighter Pilots have to have sharp eyes -

Who doesn't belong here?

ANSWER – 53 ---- TRIVIA - --

PUZZLE 5
NAME – RANK and SERIAL NUMBER

NAME QUIZ – Can You identify the Rank, Service and Country that the people listen on the Next Page held during WWII?

NAME QUIZ ANSWER CLUES

Answers include:

RANKS

1 – Sergeant
1 - Lieutenant / Captain
2 – Brigadier Generals
8 – Generals
2 – Lieutenant Generals
1 - General of the Army
5 – Field Marshals
1 – Air Marshal
3 – Air Chief Marshals
1 – Vice Admiral
2 – Admirals
1 – Rear Admiral
2 – Grand Admirals
4 – Fleet Admirals
2 – Admirals of the Fleet

NATIONALITIES

15 – Americans
7 – British
5 – Germans
3 - Japanese
2 – Dutch
1 – Canadian
1 – Australian
1 – New Zealander
1 - Free French

SERVICES

16 – ARMY
12 – NAVY
8 – AIR FORCE

ANSWER – 54 ---- TRIVIA - 85

NAME QUIZ – Can You identify the Rank, Service and Country that these people held during WWII?

PUZZLE 5

NAME	RANK	COUNTRY / SERVICE
Audie Murphy		
George Marshall		
Alan Brooke		
Charles Portal		
Omar Bradley		
Hideki Tojo		
Paul Tibbets		
Bernard Montgomery		
Bill Mauldin		
Mark Clark		
Charles de Gaulle		
Alfred Pound		
Karl Donitz		
Douglas MacArthur		
Arthur Harris		
Earnest King		
Andrew Cunningham		
Hugh Dowding		
Ira C Eaker		
William Halsey jr.		
Vernon Sturdy		
Keith Park		
Isoroku Yamamoto		
George Patton		
Conrad Helfrich		
Carl Spaatz		
Karel Doorman		
Chester Nimitz		
Andrew McNaughton		
Gerd von Rundstedt		
Raymond Spruance		
Albert Kesselring		
Dwight Eisenhower		
Erwin Rommel		
Soemu Toyoda		
Eric Raeder		

PUZZLE 6 - 1 OF 2
CHRYPTOGRAMS – US NAVY QUOTES

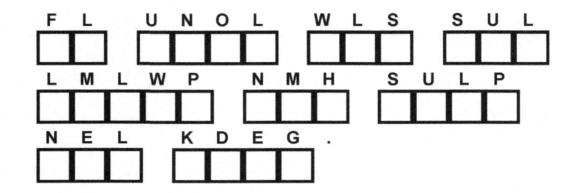

Clues: **Commander Oliver Hazard Perry**

S = T

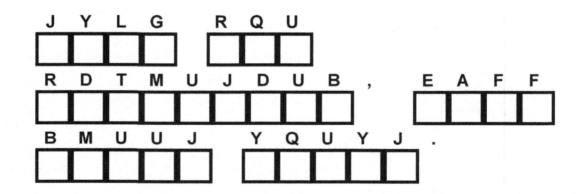

Clues: **Admiral David G. Farragut**

Y = A

ANSWER – 55 ---- TRIVIA - --

PUZZLE 6 - 2 OF 2

CHRYPTOGRAMS – US NAVY QUOTES

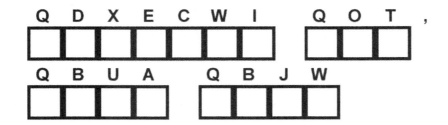

Clues: US Navy Pilot Donald Mason 1942 – Shortest victory message of all time.

B = A

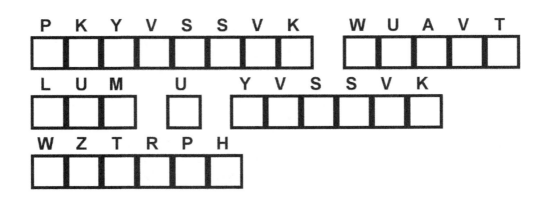

Clues: Admiral Chester A. Nimitz, Iwo Jima 1945

S = M

PUZZLE 7
ANDREW JACKSON'S 1862 VALLEY CAMPAIGN
THROUGH THE SHENANDOAH VALLEY IN VIRGINIA DURING THE AMERICAN CIVIL WAR

Follow Jackson's path

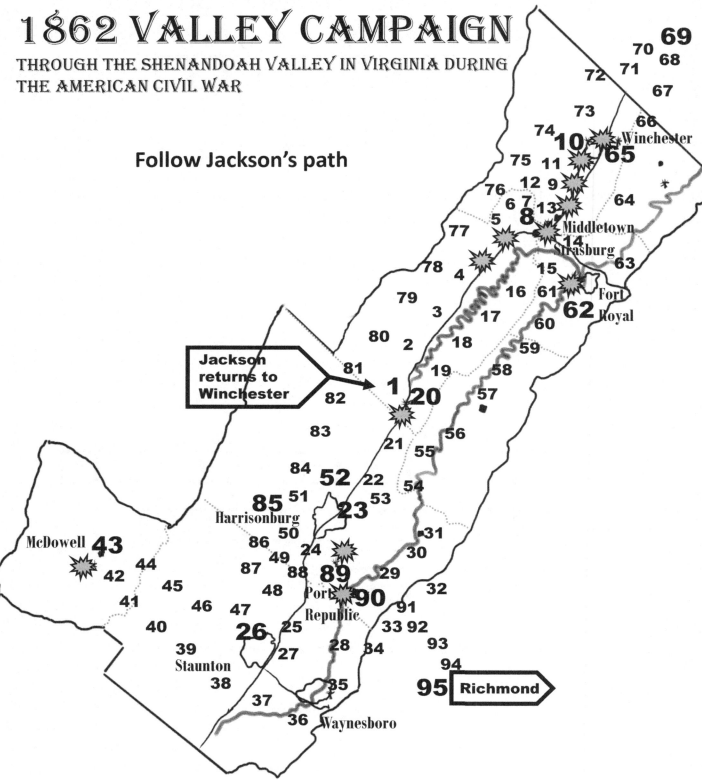

ANSWER – 56 ---- TRIVIA - 86

PUZZLE 8   FAMOUS U.S. BATTLES

How well do you know your military history - Identify the Battle

ANSWER – 57 ---- TRIVIA - 87

PUZZLE 8 — FAMOUS U.S. BATTLES

Across

3. April 1861 - Started the Civil War
4. February - March 1945 - Mount Suribachi
8. June 1944 - Last great carrier battle
11. July 1898 - Victory for the Rough Riders
12. May 1942 - First battle between Aircraft Carriers ___ Sea
13. January - July 1968 - Big battle Khe?
14. August 1942 - February 1943 - An Island NOT a waterway
16. April - May 1862 - Not the Siege of New York City
18. June 1944 - Greatest Amphibious Invasion
19. June 1942 - Exactly In Between
23. September 1950 - Turning point - Amphibious Invasion
24. August - September 1950 - UN Last Stand - Pusan _____
25. October 1944 - MacArthur returns
27. January - August 1945 - Large Philippine Island
28. April 2003 - Suddam's capital
29. June 1876 - both Big and Little

Down

1. December 1944 - January 1945 - Nuts
2. April 1775 - and Concord
5. April - June 1945 - Island Battle - Operation Iceberg
6. May 1775 - Fort on Lake Champlain
7. February - March 1836 - Remembered
9. December 1941 - Day of Infamy
10. June 1775 - _____ Hill
14. July 1863 - Lee's Waterloo
15. September 1862 - AKA Sharpsburg
17. January - May 1944 - Mountain Assault
20. September - October 1777 - Two battles 18 days apart in the Champlain Valley
21. January 1968 - Holiday Attack
22. January - June 1944 - In Italy
26. March 2003 - War
28. March 2008 - MiTTs and ETTs Operation Charge of the Knights

PUZZLE 9 Normandy Invasion
WORD SEARCH

```
L D L R V W T G C N N M B K S R A A F R G G V G Z Y T Y
E M L N L Y K H Q Y T R D U K J B M R L Z L P L Z V R X
M L Q R G K E D K X J J O K L L V K G J P Y V S T L M L
M D Y T Q R Z R J N X I T N D L M Y N M B Y C W R M G M
O D W M B T R Y I N B V V N R L E M N V L R Z Y K J T X
R V M O Y R J A Y I T D Z Y Y T P D K P E K N B V Q N Q
B M U N B X R V H L Y E P B T W R Y E A G V M Y X B K M
N R M Q T T Q P Z R C N E N B W A K M B J D L P X P D X
G A N R Y D M J D N E D C N G D Q I V W K L P B X L D T
J F H K P A N L A X V W R Y V M N F O R T R E S S N Z T
T A S A Q Z L R T W E L O D R G M D R O W S J U N O L W
Y L R T M J F R L N Z X F H R R G N I D N A L W Q D T B
L A Q Z J O M N G R E Y P E N J E W R E D N A M M O C L
M I W B N L B R P V L M A E A E M B Q M B M D N R J L N
D S F G T R M N Z N N G D L D G S O L B H K K T L L D R
P E A D D L R W P J L L L R B I B I N U R A G N O T Z X
A L Z L S I E A M E D R N R A R T K E T M A T R W R J L
T G N O Q U R V S R A N I L K B T I C P G N D U L D K W
H R R G N A X Q E M O T R R V D M B O H J O Y L Y D J Z
F Z Q N C B W P E S A R R G K D W O D N U X M K E N T D
I V R H M R K R R I O V E R B P G N B R A R Z E D Y N R
N N U K B M I B N P M O L C W Q J N T L O R C M R X X N
D T N N Z C A D A N A C R J I Y Q L L Z L L Y H T Y Q B
E D R P A N N J T G B P L J B C B L P Q K T R Q I N B W
R T T N N T T L T M B X L D D P K Y W V V Y D E G L P W
T Y S M G T J G V T B R G D D N N T V Y D L Q J V T L J
T Y Z T Q N B L Y J J M X X R T J B W N R B G X Y O Z G
```

FRANCE
OVERLORD
US
BRITAIN
CANADA
RAAF
RNZAF
PARACHUTE
BOMBARDMENT
SWORD
GOLD
OMAHA
JUNO
UTAH
CICERO
EXPEDITIONARY
SKYTRAIN
D-DAY

PATHFINDER
RIDGWAY
TONGA
FORCE
COMMANDER
EISENHOWER
MONTGOMERY
BRADLEY
ROMMEL
BEDELL
MULBERRY
LANDING
AMPHIBIOUS
ROOSEVELT
CHURCHILL
FORTRESS
FALAISE
CHERBOURG
SCREAMING-EAGLES

ANSWER – 58 ---- TRIVIA - 88

21

PUZZLE 10

MILITARY - PRESIDENTS - QUIZ

Which Presidents served in the Military?
What Branch of the Service did they serve in?
Did they hold the rank of General?

John Adams
Military Service? Y / N
Branch? – Army, Navy
          Air Force, Marines
General? Y / N

Andrew Jackson
Military Service? Y / N
Branch? – Army, Navy
          Air Force, Marines
General? Y / N

George H.W. Bush
Military Service? Y / N
Branch? – Army, Navy
          Air Force, Marines
General? Y / N

Rutherford B. Hayes
Military Service? Y / N
Branch? – Army, Navy
          Air Force, Marines
General? Y / N

James Garfield
Military Service? Y / N
Branch? – Army, Navy
          Air Force, Marines
General? Y / N

Teddy Roosevelt
Military Service? Y / N
Branch? – Army, Navy
          Air Force, Marines
General? Y / N

W.H. Harrison
Military Service? Y / N
Branch? – Army, Navy
          Air Force, Marines
General? Y / N

Millard Filmore
Military Service? Y / N
Branch? – Army, Navy
          Air Force, Marines
General? Y / N

Richard Nixon
Military Service? Y / N
Branch? – Army, Navy
          Air Force, Marines
General? Y / N

Abraham Lincoln
Military Service? Y / N
Branch? – Army, Navy
          Air Force, Marines
General? Y / N

Grover Cleveland
Military Service? Y / N
Branch? – Army, Navy
          Air Force, Marines
General? Y / N

Herbert Hoover
Military Service? Y / N
Branch? – Army, Navy
          Air Force, Marines
General? Y / N

ANSWER – 59 ---- TRIVIA - 89

WWII AIR COMBAT
Think Fast or Die!

PUZZLE 11

ONLY SHOOT DOWN ENEMY AIRCRAFT

ANSWER – 60 ---- TRIVIA - --

PUZZLE 12

HERACLITUS CRYPTOGRAM

ONE Quote in FOUR Parts

Heraclitus lived in Ephesus, an important city on the Ionian coast of Asia Minor, not far from Miletus, the birthplace of philosophy from c.(535 BC – 475 BC). He was a Greek philosopher, known for his doctrine of change being central to the universe.

The following Quote about the military is attributed to Heraclitus (though some say erroneously). The quote is broken into four parts each with its own Cryptogram.

ANSWER – 61 ---- TRIVIA - --

PUZZLE 12

"Out of every one hundred men:

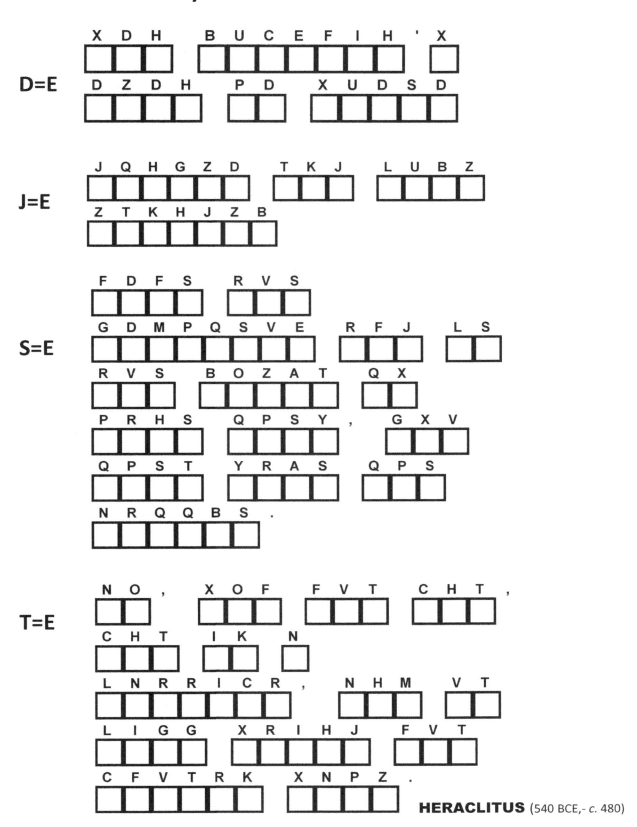

HERACLITUS (540 BCE,- c. 480)

PUZZLE 13

WAR IN AFGHANISTAN

ANSWER – 62 ---- TRIVIA - --

PUZZLE 13

WAR IN AFGHANISTAN

Across
1 2001 Invasion by US - supported by Britain and
3 US Presidents -George W. Bush and
7 Australian Prime Ministers - Howard, Rudd, Gillard and
8 US General - T. ___
10 Invasion aimed at dismantling al-
12 Rebels already fighting the Taliban - The ___ Alliance
14 Interim Afghan President
15 Pashto Grand Assembly - "loya ___
16 Afgan governement was considered the most ___ in the world.
17 War to win the ___ and minds
19 IED - ___ Explosive Device
20 British Operation Lastay-Kulang (___ Handle)

Down
2 _____ Countries Joined later
4 British Prime Ministers - Blair, Brown and
5 German Chancellors - Schroder and
6 Canadian Prime Ministers - Chretien, Martin and
9 US Secretary of Defense - D.
11 In power in Afghanistan
13 Taliban were supported by
18 UN Mandated force

PUZZLE 14

Famous PILOTS and the PLANES they flew MATCHING GAME

Match the Famous American pilot to the planes they flew

Colonel James 'Jimmy' Stewart	Grumman TBM Avenger
General Jimmy Doolittle	F4F-3 Wildcat
Lt-Col Charles Older	SOC Seagull / I-15, I-16 Polikarpov
Captain Christopher Magee	Boulton Paul Defiant – Target Tug
Lt-Col Nancy Harkness Love	C-54 / B-25 / B-17 ++++++
Frank Glasgow 'Salty Tinker	Spitfire / P-51, / Aero Shrike Commander
Lt. George 'Skin" Bush	B-17 / B-29 Superfortress
Maj. Richard Ira Bong	P-51 Mustang
Captain Claire Chennault	F4U Corsair
Brig. Gen Paul Tibbets	F4F Wildcat / F6F Hellcat / F8F Bearcat
1st Lt. Robert 'Bob Hoover	Curtiss H-75
Lt. Col. Alexander Jefferson	Wright Model B / Burgess Model H
Ola Mildred 'Sexy Rexy' 'Millie' Rexroat	P-40 Tomahawk / B-26 Invader
General Henry 'Hap' Arnold	P-38 Lightning
Maj Greg 'Pappy' Boyington	P-40B Tomahawk / F4U Corsair
Navy Capt. Roy 'Butch' Voris	B-25 Mitchell
Lt. Commander Edward 'Butch O'Hare	B-24 Liberator

ANSWER – 63 ---- TRIVIA - 90

PUZZLE 15

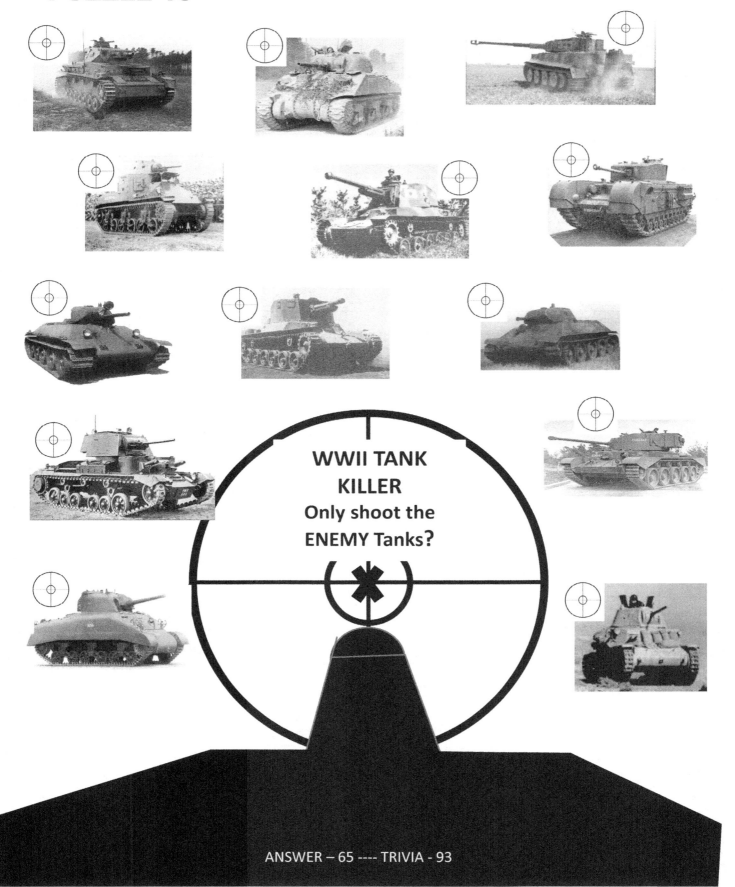

WWII TANK KILLER
Only shoot the ENEMY Tanks?

ANSWER – 65 ---- TRIVIA - 93

PUZZLE 16 – WWII HISTORY

Match the Event with the Date -

Japan Invades Manchuria	1	September 18, 1931
Italy invades Ethiopia	2	October 2, 1936
Germany and Italy - create Axis	3	October 25, 1936
Germany and Japan sign anti-communist pact	4	November 25, 1936
Japan invades China	5	July 7, 1937
Munich Agreement	6	September 29, 1938
Italy invades Albania	7	April 7, 1939
Germany invades Poland	8	September 1, 1939
France and Britain declare war on Germany	9	September 3, 1939
Soviet Union invades Poland	10	September 17, 1939
Germany invades Norway and Denmark	11	April 9, 1940
Germany attacks the low countries	12	May 10, 1940
Italy invades France	13	June 10, 1940
Italy invades British controlled Egypt	14	September 13, 1940
Germany, Italy and Japan form Tripartite pact	15	September 27, 1940
Germany sends Africa Corps to North Africa	16	February 1941
Slovakia, Hungary, Romania join Axis	17	November 20, 1941
Japan attacks Pearl Harbor	18	December 7, 1941
US Declares war on Japan	19	December 8, 1941
Axis declares war on the United States	20	December 11, 1941
Battle of Midway	21	June 1942
Germany invades Russia	22	June 28, 1942
Battle of El Alamein	23	October 23, 1942
Russians trap German 6th army - Stalingrad	24	November 23, 1942
Italy surrenders	25	September 8, 1943
Salerno Landing	26	September 9, 1943
Anzio Landing	27	January 22, 1944
Rome liberated	28	June 4, 1944
Normandy Landing	29	June 6, 1944
Southern France Landing	30	August 15, 1944
Paris Liberated	31	August 20, 1944
Philippines Landing	32	October 29, 1944
Battle of the Bulge	33	December 16, 1944
Allies cross the Rhine	34	March 7, 1945
Germany Surrenders	35	May 7, 1945
Okinawa taken	36	May 1945
Atomic Bomb dropped on Hiroshima	37	August 6, 1945
Soviet Union invades Manchuria	38	August 8, 1945
Atomic Bomb dropped on Nagasaki	39	August 9, 1945
Japan Surrenders ANSWER – 66 ---- TRIVIA - --	40	September 2, 1945

PUZZLE 17
CHRYPTOGRAMS – GEORGE S. PATTON QUOTES

1 OF 2

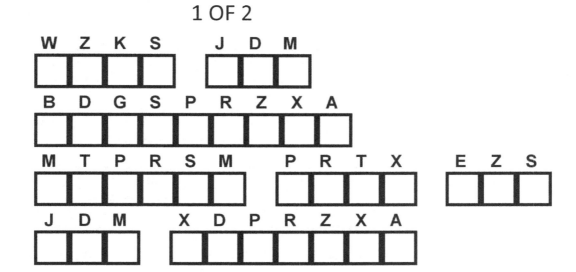

Clues:

Z = I

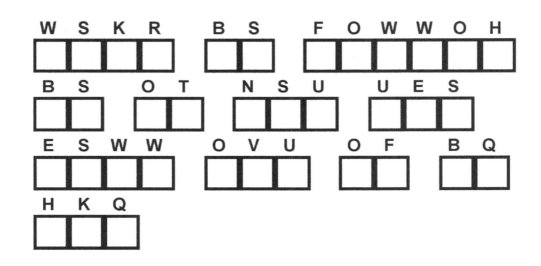

Clues:

S = E

PUZZLE 17
CHRYPTOGRAMS – GEORGE S. PATTON QUOTES
2 OF 2

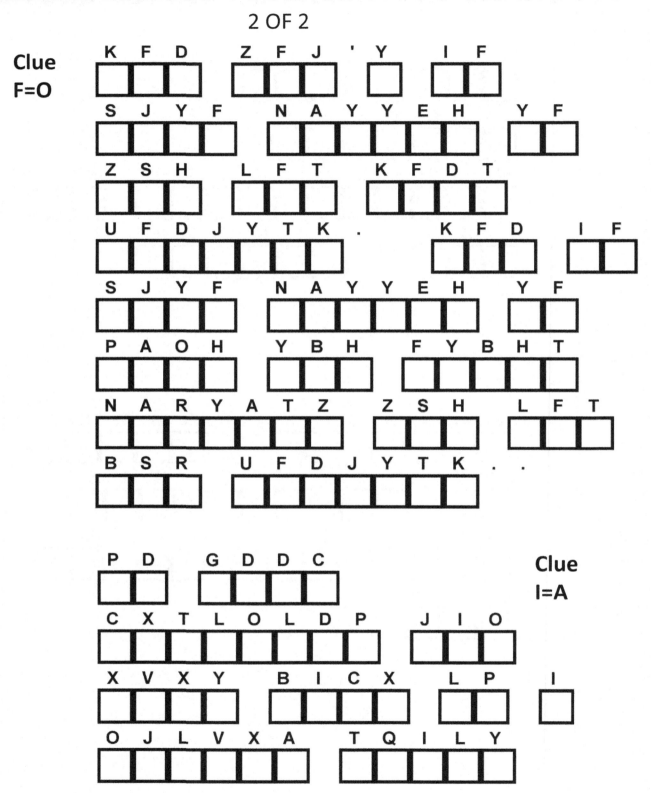

ANSWER – 67 ---- TRIVIA - --

PUZZLE 18

VIETNAM WAR

ANSWER – 68 ---- TRIVIA - --

PUZZLE 18

VIETNAM WAR

Across
2 Fought in Vietnam, Cambodia and
3 National Liberation Front- Viet
5 Reliance on Ground forces, Artillery and
6 Spread of Communism - _____ Theory
7 1964 -Gulf of ___ Incident
9 US Gradual withdrawal called -
10 1973 Fall of
12 Use of B52 bombers loaded with nuclear weapons at the edge of Soviet airspace- 'The ____Theory'
15 1970 - US and ARVN troops invade
18 Negotiated for peace - Henry

Down
1 AKA Second _____ War
4 Peoples Army of Vietnam
8 1968 major offensive
11 1969 - Build up of South Vietnamese Forces - ____ Doctrine
13 US Theater Commander - Creighton ____
14 Nixon - "The ____ Majority' supports the war
16 '____ Papers' uncovered
17 North Vietnamese trail through Laos - Ho-Chi ___
19 1972 massive bombing of Hanoi and Haipong - Operation ____

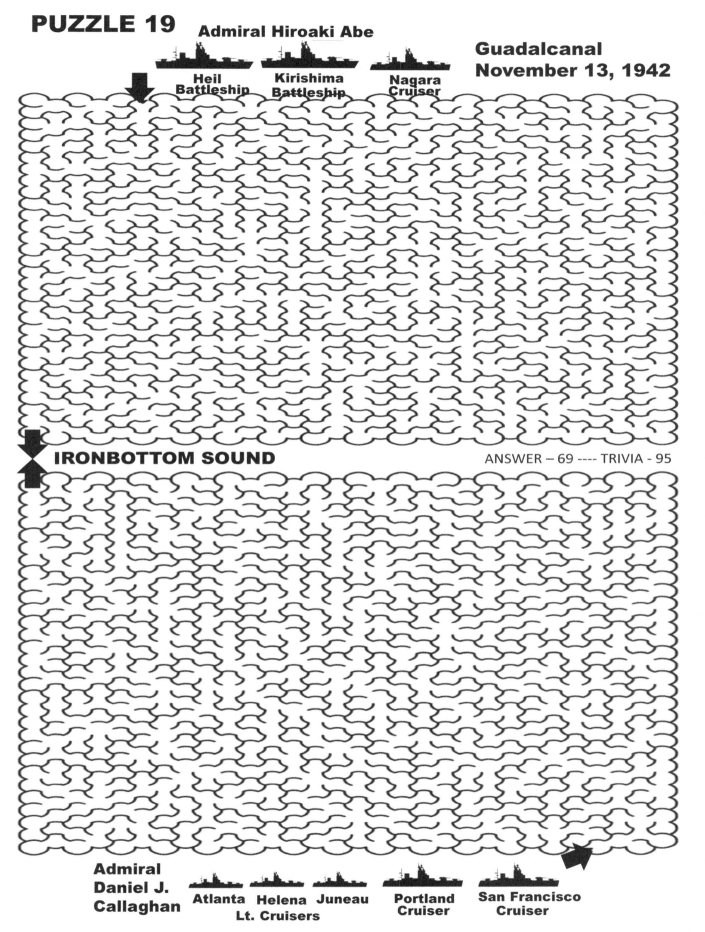

PUZZLE 20 – WWI - QUIZ

Which came first – Put the events in order (Start Dates)

	Battle of the Somme	1	June 28, 1914
	Wilson calls for "peace without victory'	2	August 1914
	Selective Service Act passed	3	August 4, 1914
	Battle of Sedan	4	August 4, 1914
	Second Battle of the Marne	5	August 21, 1914
	Battle of Neuve Chapelle	6	August 23, 1914
	Battle of Vimy Ridge	7	October 19, 1914
	Nations Align (Axis) vs (Allies)	8	March 10, 1915
	US Declares War on Germany	9	May 7, 1915
	Battle of Passchendaele	10	February 21, 1916
	Battle of Belleau Wood	11	July 1, 1916
	Archduke Ferdinand assassinated	12	January 22, 1917
	Battle of Cantigny	13	April 6, 1917
	Lusitania Sunk	14	April 9, 1917
	Germany Surrenders	15	May 28, 1917
	Third Battle of Ypres	16	July 31, 1917
	Battle and Siege of Liege	17	October, 12, 1917
	Battle of Verdun	18	January 1918
	Battle of Meuse-Argonne	19	May 28, 1918
	US Declares Neutrality	20	June 1918
	Battle of Mons	21	July 1918
	Wilson suggests League of Nations	22	September 1918
	Battle of the Ardennes	23	October 1918
	First Battle of Ypres	24	November 11, 1918

ANSWER – 70 ---- TRIVIA - --

PUZZLE 21
Marine Words

```
Q C J N N J X G E E D U N K L C P L I C
N U N Z N L A J G N S A H P L A B P N J
Z M Q M Q T L R A T R M I L X Y W X Q Z
Y S L L D G R L H L P L Y M R A Z R G P
X H J K Y Z Y T Y E L C D L X D B M D K
H A D X Q E B J R E A V S E M P E R F I
O W W D N W B L T N R D C A S E V A C L
M L N S V Y M A O T A C Z N V Y Z Q E T
E Y I V D T K E R E T N A Y C X N A Y G
S D Z D W C U D H N W G T V L O T N Y L
L A Y L U V E K N Y E Y A J E H N Y U D
I L L M Z C L V L Y Y Y Y N E D Z U Y G
C I H X K U R Q H V R P S R G A E T S R
E C Y Y B N Y B A A D E N T M W F M L D
S E T O O B K N K V R E P T Y K A M T Z
L X G L P N L J Y Z C O B O T L Y Y V W
T D Q D N W Z Y Z K L K O W O L E M W G
G T M R K B Y T R Y T R Y L N L T T L D
G B G D Q R Z X N X D T Y P N B B L X G
```

ANSWER — 71 ---- TRIVIA - 97

ALICE
BLOOPER
CANOEU
CONUS
Disneyland
Gangway
Leatherneck
Homeslice
LCPLIC
NAVY
Deck
Schmuckatelli
OORAH

Boot
CASEVAC
BarneyStyle
ALPHAS
ARMY
Bulkhead
Cumshaw
Gunny
Jarhead
MEDEVAC
VMFA
Geedunk
SemperFi

37

PUZZLE 22

FAMOUS GENERALS - MATCHING GAME –
Match the US Generals with their Middle names or Nicknames

George Washington	Armstrong
Winfield Scott	Catlett
Robert Lee	Miller
Ulysses Grant	The Grand Old Man of the Army
John Pershing	Fighting Joe
Dwight Eisenhower	Bunker
George Patton	Smith
Douglas MacArthur	Herbert
Matthew Ridgway	Johnathan
Norman Schwarzkopf	David
Joseph Hooker	Hiram
Earnest Hemingway	William
Thomas 'Stonewall' Jackson	Joseph
James Mattis	Gaijin Shogun
George Custer	Old Fox
Chester Nimitz	Marse
George Marshall	Norman

ANSWER – 72 ---- TRIVIA - 98

PUZZLE 23
QUOTES from WWI, and KOREA

```
I Q K I Q F K ?   R Q J J ,
H Q   Z G P K   M T K
R Q I Q .
```
Clue K=T

Marine Capt. Lloyd Williams – Belleau Wood - WWI

Clue H=O
```
Z H   A E P B   Z H   A R H T J
```

Major General Frederick C. Blesse - KOREA

```
Z J X   K F R C V W G L !
H A F I D W !
```
Clue W=E
```
W B W I R K C E R   D C W L
O J G A   M W !
```

Captain Lewis Millett - KOREA

ANSWER – 73 ---- TRIVIA - --

PUZZLE 24

WWII FACTS – FILL-IN –THE BLANKS WESTERN EUROPE

	ANSWERS
April – November 1941 - Western Desert Campaign – Siege of _____	Alamein
July 1942 - Western Desert Campaign – Battle of El _____	Ranger
July 1940 - Italian Invasion of _____	Ortona
Feb. 1943 – Tunisia - 1st Major US -Axis battle – Battle of _____ Pass.	Britain
23 March 1943 - Tunisia – First US Victory over Axis - Battle of El _____	Norway
23 March – Tunisia – US Commander at El Guetter Pass - _____	Rhine
23 March – Unit critical to operations in El Guetter – 1st _____ Battalion	Market
June 1940 – December 1942 – Siege of the Island of _____	Luxembourg
April 1941 – German invasion of _____	Italy
July – August 1943 – Battle of _____	Kasserine
September 1943 – Operation Slapstick – Invasion of _____	Malta
December 1943 – Easter Coast of Italy - Battle of _____	Tobruk
December 1943 – Bernhardt Line – Monte La Difensa - _____ Brigade	Devil's
January thru May 1944 – West Coast of Italy – Battle of Monte _____	Cassino
January 22, 1944 – Allied Amphibious Landing – Battle of _____	Liberation
September 13-24, 1944 – Greek/Canadian/New Zealanders – Battle of _____	Rimini
April -June 1940, Europe – Axis Invasion of _____	Anzio
May 1940 – Europe – Axis Invasion of Belgium, Netherlands and _____	Greece
26 May – June 4, 1940 – evacuation of _____	Dunkerque
July – October 1940 – In the Air – Battle of _____	Eisenhower
June 6, 1944 – Return to Continental Europe – Operation _____	Overlord
June 6, 1944 – Normandy Invasion Commander - _____	Bulge
August 25, 1944 - _____ of Paris	Sicily
17-25 September, 1944 – Operation _____ Garden	Patton
December 1944 to January 1945 – Easter Belgium – Battle of the _____	Sudan
March 24 1945 – U.S. XVIII Airborne / British 6th Airborne cross the _____	Guettar
ANSWER – 74 ---- TRIVIA - --	

PUZZLE 25 # WWII Battles

```
S P E A R L V S J I J J X T D N
E X M B W L I C D T N Y R P B M
N Q P B T C Z I Y A W D I M M V
I R Z M I V M T D L L D D X L Y
P K O L W D V N T Y J T N B R X
P A Y D L A N A C L A D A U G C
I S D L I J B L A G T L B R A P
L S R N Z G R T R N X Y E S E N
I E O M E T E A Y T Z T S L T V
H R L Y L D B R N E T I E P M Y
P I R K M A R I R E N L O P D L
X N E B U A E A U O I I G B X K
K E V L U M R G G U C Y H Y N D
M M O W A L T K L J N G B R N N
Z N M L R K G R E Z Z Y M Z Y N
W L A T M D N E Z T X Z V Q K G
```

Alamein
Kasserine
Guetter
Sicily
Italy
Cassino
Anzio
Overlord
Market
Garden

Bulge
Rhine
Atlantic
Pearl
Philippines
Corregidor
Rabaul
Midway
Guadalcanal
Peleliu

ANSWER — 75 ---- TRIVIA - --

PUZZLE 26 DOG FIGHT
Where will they meet?

ANSWER – 76 ---- TRIVIA - --

PUZZLE 27

CHRYPTOGRAMS – QUOTES BY GENERALS

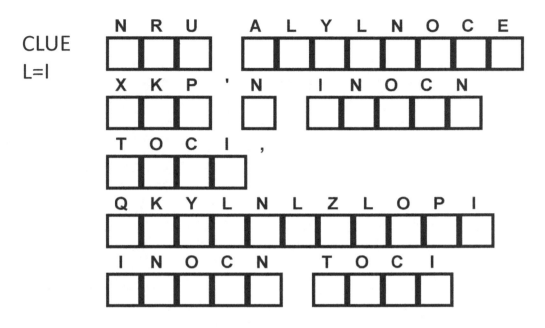

General William C. Westmoreland

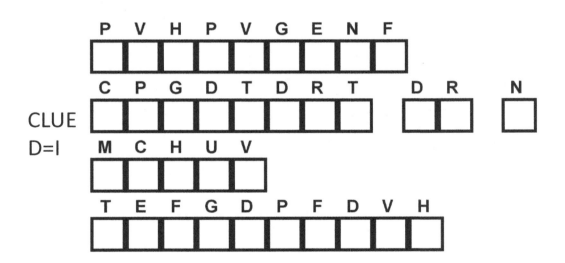

General Colin Powell

PUZZLE 27

CHRYPTOGRAMS – QUOTES BY GENERALS

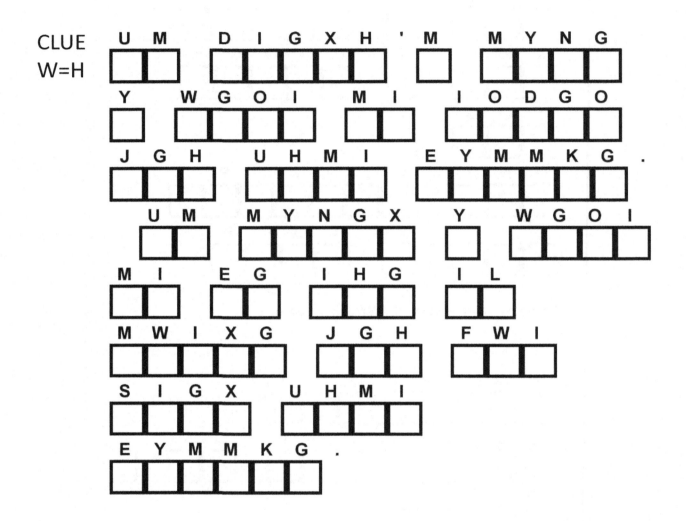

General H. Norman Schwarzkopf

ANSWER – 50 ---- TRIVIA - 82

PUZZLE 28
FRIEND or FOE

ANSWER – 78 ---- TRIVIA - 100

PUZZLE 29 – WWII - - OCEAN WAR

FILL-IN-THE BLANKS

Fill-in-the-Blanks	ANSWERS
1939 – 1945 Battle of the _____ September 1939 – Battle of the River _____ February 16 1940 – HMS Cossack frees prisoners from the German tanker _____ 24 May 1941 – HMS Hood sunk and HMS Prince of Wales damaged by Bismarck and Prinz _____ July 1942 Convoy PQ 17 lost 24 of 35 ships while heading for the Russian Port of _____ Cruisers HMS Sheffield and Jamaica vs Cruisers Lutzow and Hipper - Battle of the _____ Sea December 1943 – RN with HMS Duke of York sinks Battleship Scharnhorst. Battle of North_____ Only American Battleship at the landing at Casablanca – USS _____ Aircraft carriers at Casablanca landing – Suwannee and _____ 300nmi west of Brest France -_____ sunk. Torpedo Alley off the coast of North _____ 5 May 1945 - Last US flagged ship sunk during the war. SS _____ Point 6 May 1945 -USS Ericsson, Amick, Atherton & Moberly; Blimps K-16 & K-58 sink U-853 off Pt. _____ December 7, 1941 _____ Harbor. December 1941- Battles of Wake and _____ June 1942 – Japanese occupation of _____ January – April 1942 – Japanese invasion of The _____ MacArthur consolidated his Philippine forces at Bataan and the island of _____ Straight where HMAS Perth and USS Houston were sunk._____ Port in Territory of New Guinea – Battle of _____ May 1942 – Battle of the Coral _____ June 1942 – Battle of _____ Hint -Neither Here nor There AKA; Battle of Solomon Sea, Battle of Friday the 13th, Battle of _____ Aug 6,7 1943 – Destroyers vs Destroyers – Battle of _____ Gulf September – November 1944 – Operation Stalemate – Marines' most bitter battle*. _____ October – December 1944 – MacArthur returns – Battle of _____ Five Weeks in February and March 1945 – Joe Rosenthal's famous picture - _____ ANSWER – 79 ---- TRIVIA - --	Barents Atlantic Ranger Cape Massachusetts Bismarck Pearl Black Judith Carolina Iwo Jima Sunda Kiska Corregidor Leyte Guam Vella Peleliu Rabaul Arkangelsk Guadalcanal Philippines Midway Altmark Plate Eugen Sea

PUZZLE 30

- CHRYPTOGRAMS -
REVOLUTION AND CIVIL WAR

Clue
A=E

L N   S U A F   B A J K   S X

U J G A   J   Z J V ,   T A S

L S   C A D L K   U A V A !

Captain John Parker Lexington April 19, 1775

Clue
O=I

H W S   O E   C X G G

General William Tecumseh Sherman

Clue
Z=I

B O D Q D   Z Y

P S T V Y G E

Y B S E H Z E C   X Z V D   S

Y B G E D   I S X X .

Brigadier General Barnard Elliot Bee – At Bull Run

ANSWER – 80 ---- TRIVIA - --

ANSWERS

ACES - ANSWERS

PUZZLE 1

Name	ACE Y/N	Nationality	Victories
Eric Hartmann	Y	GERMANY	352
Gregory Boyington	Y	AMERICA	28
Hosato Takei	N	AMERICA	
Hans Wind	Y	FINLAND	75
Aleksandr Pokryshkin	Y	USSR	59
Robert Stanford Tuck	Y	BRITAIN	30
David Deihl	N	AMERICA	
Eino Luukkanen	Y	FINLAND	56
Eric Rudorffer	Y	GERMAN	222
Michael Faraday	N	BRITAIN	
Shoichi Sugita	Y	JAPAN	70
Roger Sherman	N	AMERICAN	
David Campbell	Y	AMERICAN	34
Richard I. Bong	Y	AMERICAN	40
Shigeo Fukumoto	Y	JAPAN	72
Yully Borisovich	N	AMERICAN	
Jari Kurri	N	FINLAND	
Harold Scherer	N	AMERICAN	
Spencer Chaplin	N	BRITAIN	
Nevil Duke	Y	BRITAIN	27
Ivan Koshedub	Y	USSR	66

PUZ - 2 - US MILITARY GENERAL KNOWLEDGE - ANSWERS

How much do you know about the US Military?

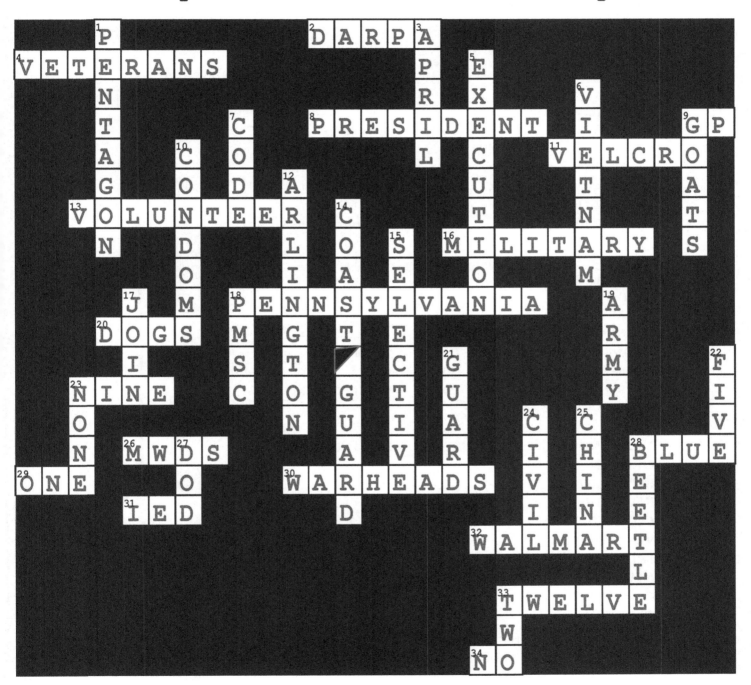

PUZ 3 – BATTLESHIP QUIZ - ANSWERS

BATTLESHIP?	YES	NO	AMERICAN? NOT A BATTLESHIP?	YES	NO
COLORADO	X			X	
FLORIDA	X			X	
ALASKA		X	Cruiser	X	
INDIANA	X			X	
BARHAM	X		Great Britain		X
KEARSARGE	X			X	
WEST VIRGINIA	X			X	
DALE		X	USN Destroyer	X	
WYOMING	X			X	
HAWAII		X	Submarine (SSN-776)	X	
OHIO	X			X	
AMERICA		X	****	X	
HOWE	X		Great Britain		X
CENTURION	X		Great Britain		X
MONTANA		X	Submarine (SSN-794)		
TIRPITZ	X		Germany		X
ST LOUIS		X	USN Lt Cruiser	x	
DAUNTLESS		X	RN Cruiser		X
DENVER		X	USN Lt Cruiser	X	
TEXAS	X			X	
IOWA	X			X	
PROVENCE	X		FRANCE		X
CONGRESS		X	*****	x	
DETROIT		X	USN Lt Cruiser	X	
VIRGINIA	X			X	
UTAH	X			X	
INDEPENDENCE		X	USN Lt Carrier	X	
OREGON	X			X	
BENNINGTON		X	USN Carrier	X	
REVENGE	X		Great Britain		X
CONSTITUTION		X	*****	x	
WASHINGTON	X			X	
FREEDOM		X	******	x	
NEW YORK	X			X	
CANBERRA		X	USN Hvy Cruiser	X	
ALABAMA	X			X	

**** AMERICA – USS AMERICA – (LHA-6) A modern US Amphibious Assault Ship – USS America (CV-66) 1960s era Super Carrier

***** CONGRESS / CONSTITUTION – USS CONGRESS – AND - USS CONSTITUTION – Two of America's first six original Frigates along with the USS UNITED STATES, USS CHESAPEAKE, USS CONSTELLATION, and USS PRESIDENT.

****** FREEDOM – USS FREEDOM (LCS-1) Littoral Combat Ship – Christened September 2006 – USS Freedom (ID-3024) WWI cargo Ship – USS Freedom (IX-43) auxiliary schooner 1940-1962.

PUZ #4 - ANSWERS

Who doesn't belong here?
Beware the Zeros

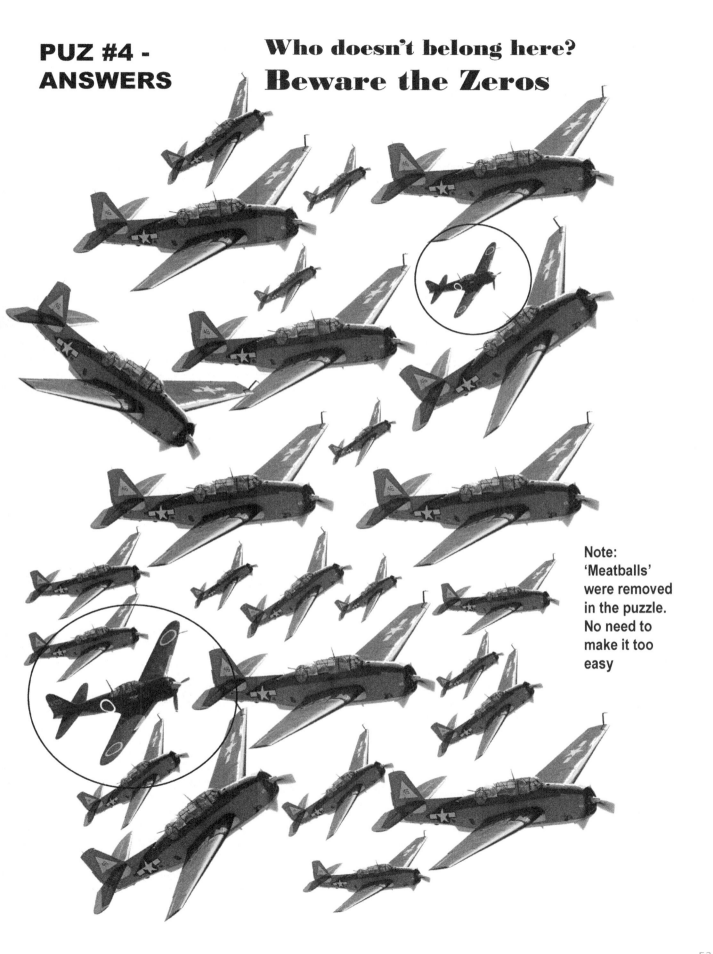

Note: 'Meatballs' were removed in the puzzle. No need to make it too easy

PUZ #5　　　NAME QUIZ ANSWERS

NAME	RANK	COUNTRY / SERVICE
Audie Murphy	1st Lieutenant / Captain	US Army / Texas National Guard
George Marshall	General / Chief of Staff / Sec of State	US Army
Alan Brooke	Field Marshal	British Army
Charles Portal	Marshal	Royal Air Force (RAF)
Omar Bradley	General	US Army
Hideki Tojo	General	Japanese Army (IJA)
Paul Tibbets	Brigadier General	US Air Force (USAF)
Bernard Montgomery	Field Marshal	British Army
Bill Mauldin	Sergeant	US Army
Mark Clark	General	US Army
Charles de Gaulle	General de Brigade	Free French Army
Alfred Pound	Admiral of the Fleet	Royal Navy (RN)
Karl Donitz	Grand Admiral	German Navy (Kriegsmarine)
Douglas MacArthur	General	US Army
Arthur Harris	Air Chief Marshal	Royal Air Force (RAF)
Earnest King	Fleet Admiral	US Navy (USN)
Andrew Cunningham	Admiral of the Fleet	Royal Navy (RN)
Hugh Dowding	Air Chief Marshal	Royal Air Force (RAF)
Ira C Eaker	General	US Army Air Force (USAAF)
William Halsey jr.	Fleet Admiral	US Navy (USN)
Vernon Sturdy	Lieutenant General	Australian Army
Keith Park	Air Chief Marshal	New Zealand Air Force (RNZAF)
Isoroku Yamamoto	Fleet Admiral	Japanese navy (IJN)
George Patton	General	US Army
Conrad Helfrich	Vice Admiral	Netherlands Navy (HNLM)
Carl Spaatz	General	US Army Air Force (USAAF)
Karel Doorman	Rear Admiral	Netherlands Navy (HNLM)
Chester Nimitz	Fleet Admiral	US Navy (USN)
Andrew McNaughton	Lieutenant General	Canadian Army (RCA)
Gerd von Rundstedt	Field Marshal	German Army (Wehrmacht)
Raymond Spruance	Admiral	US Navy (USN)
Albert Kesselring	Field Marshal	German Air Force (Luftwaffe)
Dwight Eisenhower	General of the Army	US Army
Erwin Rommel	Field Marshal	German Army (Wehrmacht)
Soemu Toyoda	Admiral	Japanese Navy (IJN)
Eric Raeder	Grand Admiral	German Navy (Kriegsmarine)

PUZ #6 - ANSWERS

CHRYPTOGRAMS – US NAVY QUOTES

"WE HAVE MET THE ENEMY AND THEY ARE OURS."

Commander Oliver Hazard Perry

"DAMN THE TORPEDOES, FULL SPEED AHEAD."

Admiral David G. Farragut

"SIGHTED SUB, SANK SAME."

US Navy Pilot Donald Mason 1942 – Shortest victory message of all time.

"UNCOMMON VALOR WAS A COMMON VIRTUE."

Admiral Chester A. Nimitz, Iwo Jima 1945

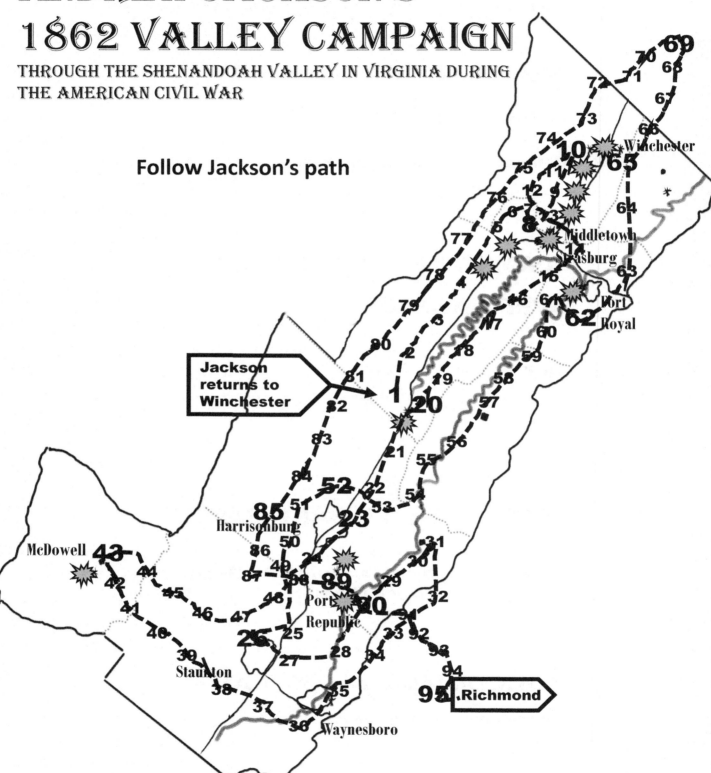

PUZ# 8 - ANSWER   FAMOUS U.S. BATTLES

How well do you know your military history - Identify the Battle

PUZ# 9 - ANSWERS
Normandy Invasion
WORD SEARCH

PUZ#10 – MILITARY / PRESIDENTS - ANSWERS

John Adams
Military Service? Y / **(N)**
Branch? – Army, Navy
  Air Force, Marines
General? Y / N

W.H. Harrison
Military Service? **(Y)** N
Branch? – **(Army)** Navy
  Air Force, Marines
General? **(Y)** N

Andrew Jackson
Military Service? **(Y)** N
Branch? – **(Army)** Navy
  Air Force, Marines
General? Y / N

Millard Filmore
Military Service? **(Y)** N
Branch? – **(Army)** Navy
  Air Force, Marines
General? Y **(N)**

George H.W. Bush
Military Service? **(Y)** N
Branch? – Army **(Navy)**
  Air Force, Marines
General? Y **(N)**

Richard Nixon
Military Service? **(Y)** N
Branch? – Army **(Navy)**
  Air Force, Marines
General? Y **(N)**

Rutherford B. Hayes
Military Service? **(Y)** N
Branch? – **(Army)** Navy
  Air Force, Marines
General? **(Y)** N

Abraham Lincoln
Military Service? **(Y)** N
Branch? – **(Army)** Navy
  Air Force, Marines
General? Y **(N)**

James Garfield
Military Service? **(Y)** N
Branch? – **(Army)** Navy
  Air Force, Marines
General? **(Y)** N

Grover Cleveland
Military Service? Y **(N)**
Branch? – Army, Navy
  Air Force, Marines
General? Y / N

Teddy Roosevelt
Military Service? **(Y)** N
Branch? – **(Army)** Navy
  Air Force, Marines
General? Y **(N)**

Herbert Hoover
Military Service? Y **(N)**
Branch? – Army, Navy
  Air Force, Marines
General? Y / N

WWII AIR COMBAT
PUZZLE 11 — ANSWER

- P-51 Mustang
- Hawker Hurricane
- P-40 Warhawk
- F4U Corsair
- Spitfire
- P47 Thunderbolt
- ZERO
- P-38 Lightning

ONLY SHOOT DOWN ENEMY AIRCRAFT

PUZ# 12 - ANSWER

HERACLITUS

"Out of every one hundred men,

Ten shouldn't even be there,

Eighty are just targets,

Nine are the real fighters, and we are lucky to have them, for they make the battle.

Ah, but the one, one is a warrior, and he will bring the others back."

PUZ# 13 - ANSWER

WAR IN AFGHANISTAN

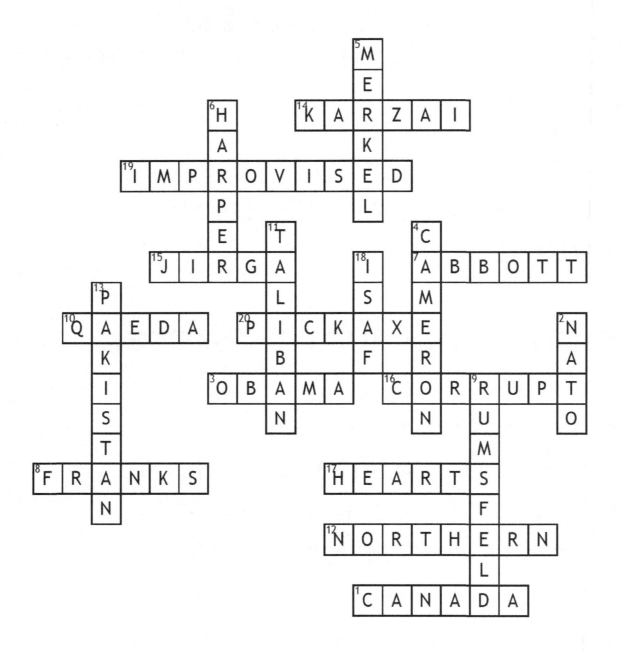

PUZ#14 - ANSWERS
Famous PILOTS and the PLANES they flew

Pilot	Plane
Colonel James 'Jimmy' Stewart	B-24 Liberator
General Jimmy Doolittle	B-25 Mitchell
Lt-Col Charles Older	P-40B Tomahawk / F4U Corsair
Captain Christopher Magee	F4U Corsair
Lt-Col Nancy Harkness Love	C-54 / B-25 / B-17 ++++++
Frank Glasgow 'Salty Tinker'	Spitfire / P-51, / Aero Shrike Commander
Lt. George 'Skin' Bush	Grumman TBM Avenger
Maj. Richard Ira Bong	P-38 Lightning
Captain Claire Chennault	P-40 Tomahawk / B-26 Invader
Brig. Gen Paul Tibbets	B-17 / B-29 Superfortress
1st Lt. Robert 'Bob' Hoover	Spitfire / P-51 / Aero Shrike Commander
Lt. Col. Alexander Jefferson	P-51 Mustang
Ola Mildred 'Sexy Rexy' 'Millie' Rexroat	SOC Seagull / I-15, I-16 Polikarpov
General Henry 'Hap' Arnold	Wright Model B / Burgess Model H
Maj Greg 'Pappy' Boyington	P-40B Tomahawk / F4U Corsair
Navy Capt. Roy 'Butch' Voris	F4F Wildcat / F6F Hellcat / F8F Bearcat
Lt. Commander Edward 'Butch' O'Hare	F4F-3 Wildcat

Famous PILOTS and the PLANES they flew ANSWERS

Colonel James 'Jimmy' Stewart → B-24 Liberator

General Jimmy Doolittle → B-25 Mitchell

Lt-Col Charles Older → P-40B Tomahawk / B-26 Invader

Captain Christopher Magee → F4U Corsair

Lt-Col Nancy Harkness Love → C-54 / B-25 / B-17 ++++++

Frank Glasgow 'Salty Tinker → SOC Seagull. I-15 and I-16 Polikarpov

Lt. George 'Skin" Bush → Grumman TBM Avenger

Maj. Richard Ira Bong → P-38 Lightning

Captain Claire Chennault → Curtis H-75

Brig. Gen Paul Tibbets → B-17 / B29 Superfortress

1st Lt. Robert 'Bob Hoover → Spitfire / P-51 / Aero Shrike Commander

Lt. Col. Alexander Jefferson → P-51 Mustang

Ola Mildred 'Sexy Rexy' 'Millie' Rexroat → Boulton Paul Defiant – Target Tug

General Henry 'Hap' Arnold → Wright Model B / Burgess Model H

Maj Greg 'Pappy' Boyington → P-40B Tomahawk / F4U Corsair

Navy Capt. Roy 'Butch' Voris → F4F Wildcat / F6F Hellcat / F8F Bearcat

Lt. Commander Edward 'Butch O'Hare → F4F-3 Wildcat

PUZ# 15 ANSWER — WWII TANK KILLER

German Panzer IV

M4 Sherman USA

German Tiger 1

M2A USA

Type 3 Chi-Nu Japan

Mk IV Churchill Britain

T34 Russia

Type 1 Ho-Ni Japan

T32 Russia

A9 Cruiser Britain

A34 Cruiser Comet Britain

M4 Sherman USA

M13 Italy

PUZ# 16 – WWII HISTORY - ANSWERS

1	Japan Invades Manchuria	1	September 18, 1931
15	Italy invades Ethiopia	2	October 2, 1936
10	Germany and Italy - create Axis	3	October 25, 1936
16	Germany and Japan sign anti-communist pact	4	November 25, 1936
25	Japan invades China	5	July 7, 1937
6	Munich Agreement	6	September 29, 1938
20	Italy invades Albania	7	April 7, 1939
11	Germany invades Poland	8	September 1, 1939
24	France and Britain declare war on Germany	9	September 3, 1939
32	Soviet Union invades Poland	10	September 17, 1939
9	Germany invades Norway and Denmark	11	April 9, 1940
38	Germany attacks the low countries	12	May 10, 1940
14	Italy invades France	13	June 10, 1940
33	Italy invades British controlled Egypt	14	September 13, 1940
26	Germany, Italy and Japan form Tripartite pact	15	September 27, 1940
36	Germany sends Africa Corps to North Africa	16	February 1941
2	Slovakia, Hungary, Romania join Axis	17	November 20, 1941
21	Japan attacks Pearl Harbor	18	December 7, 1941
27	US Declares war on Japan	19	December 8, 1941
23	Axis declares war on the United States	20	December 11, 1941
5	Battle of Midway	21	June 1942
39	Germany invades Russia	22	June 28, 1942
13	Battle of El Alamein	23	October 23, 1942
34	Russians trap German 6th army - Stalingrad	24	November 23, 1942
19	Italy surrenders	25	September 8, 1943
37	Salerno Landing	26	September 9, 1943
4	Anzio Landing	27	January 22, 1944
40	Rome liberated	28	June 4, 1944
35	Normandy Landing	29	June 6, 1944
12	Southern France Landing	30	August 15, 1944
28	Paris Liberated	31	August 20, 1944
3	Philippines Landing	32	October 29, 1944
31	Battle of the Bulge	33	December 16, 1944
8	Allies cross the Rhine	34	March 7, 1945
29	Germany Surrenders	35	May 7, 1945
22	Okinawa taken	36	May 1945
17	Atomic Bomb dropped on Hiroshima	37	August 6, 1945
18	Soviet Union invades Manchuria	38	August 8, 1945
30	Atomic Bomb dropped on Nagasaki	39	August 9, 1945
7	Japan Surrenders	40	September 2, 1945

PUZ# 17 - ANSWERS
GEORGE S. PATTON QUOTES

"LIVE FOR SOMETHING RATHER THAN DIE FOR NOTHING."

"LEAD ME, FOLLOW ME, OR GET THE HELL OUT OF MY WAY."

"YOU DON'T GO INTO BATTLE TO DIE FOR YOUR COUNTRY. YOU GO INTO BATTLE TO MAKE THE OTHER BASTARD DIE FOR HIS COUNTRY."

"NO GOOD DECISION WAS EVER MADE IN A SWIVEL CHAIR."

PUZ# 18 - ANSWERS

VIETNAM WAR

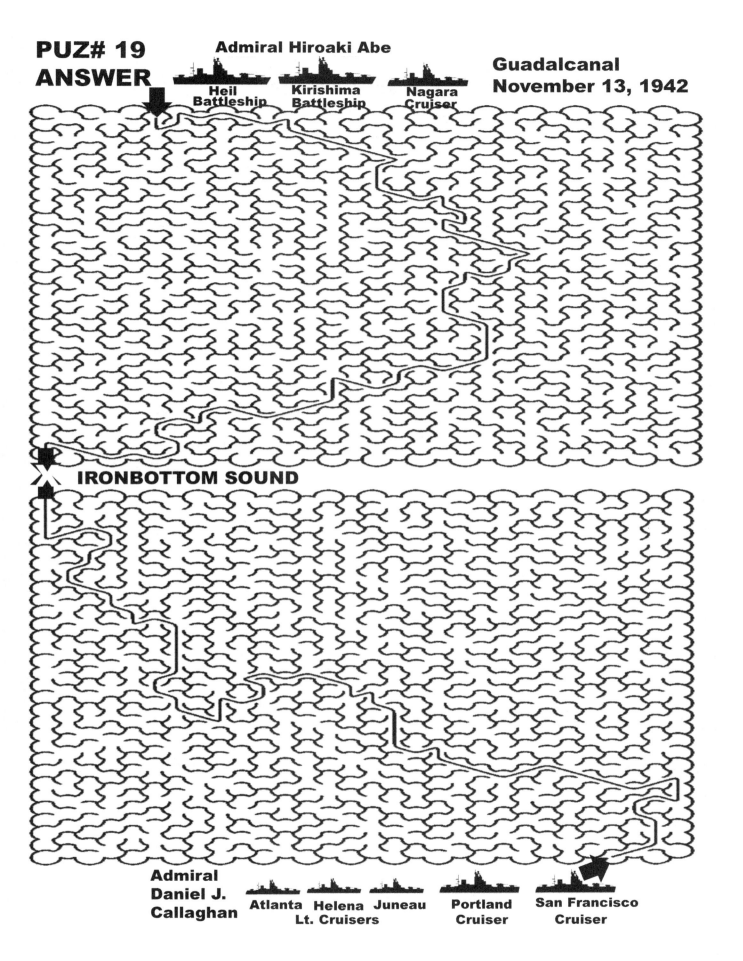

PUZ# 20 – WWI – QUIZ - ANSWERS

Which came first –. Put the events in order (Start Dates)

11	Battle of the Somme	1	June 28, 1914
12	Wilson calls for "peace without victory'	2	August 1914
15	Selective Service Act passed	3	August 4, 1914
23	Battle of Sedan	4	August 4, 1914
21	Second Battle of the Marne	5	August 21, 1914
8	Battle of Neuve Chapelle	6	August 23, 1914
14	Battle of Vimy Ridge	7	October 19, 1914
2	Nations Align (Axis) vs (Allies)	8	March 10, 1915
13	US Declares War on Germany	9	May 7, 1915
17	Battle of Passchendaele	10	February 21, 1916
20	Battle of Belleau Wood	11	July 1, 1916
1	Archduke Ferdinand assassinated	12	January 22, 1917
19	Battle of Cantigny	13	April 6, 1917
9	Lusitania Sunk	14	April 9, 1917
24	Germany Surrenders	15	May 28, 1917
16	Third Battle of Ypres	16	July 31, 1917
4	Battle and Siege of Liege	17	October, 12, 1917
10	Battle of Verdun	18	January 1918
22	Battle of Meuse-Argonne	19	May 28, 1918
3	US Declares Neutrality	20	June 1918
6	Battle of Mons	21	July 1918
18	Wilson suggests League of Nations	22	September 1918
5	Battle of the Ardennes	23	October 1918
7	First Battle of Ypres	24	November 11, 1918

PUZ# 21 ANSWERS
Marine Words

```
Q C J N N J X G E E D U N K L C P L I O
N U N Z N L A J G N S A H P L A B P N J
Z M Q M Q T L R A T R M D L X Y W X Q Z
Y S L L D G R L H L P L Y M R A Z R G P
X H J K Y Z Y T Y E O D L X D B M D K
H A D X Q E B J R E A V S E M P E R F I
O W W D N W B L T N R D C A S E V A O L
M L N S V Y M A O T A C Z N V Y Z Q E T
E Y I V D T K E R E T N A Y C X N A Y G
S D Z D W C U D H N W G T V L O T N Y L
L A Y L U V E K N Y E Y A J E H N Y U D
I L L M Z C L V L Y Y Y Y N E D Z U Y G
C I H X K U R Q H V R P S R G A E T S R
E C Y Y B N Y B A A D E N T M W F M L D
S F T O O B K N K V R E P T Y K A M T Z
L X G L P N L J Y Z C O B O T L Y Y V W
T D Q D N W Z Y Z K L K O W O L E M W G
G T M R K B Y T R Y T R Y L N L T T L D
G B G D Q R Z X N X D T Y P N B B L X G
```

PUZ# 22 - ANSWERS

FAMOUS GENERALS

Match the US Generals with their Middle names or Nicknames

George Washington	Old Fox
Winfield Scott	The Grand Old Man of the Army
Robert E. Lee	Marse Robert
Ulysses S Grant	Hiram
John J. Pershing	Joseph
Dwight D. Eisenhower	David
George S. Patton	Smith
Douglas MacArthur	Gaijin Shogun
Matthew B. Ridgway	Bunker
Norman Schwarzkopf	Herbert
Joseph Hooker	Fighting Joe
Earnest Hemingway	Miller
Thomas 'Stonewall' Jackson	Johnathan
James Mattis	Norman
George A. Custer	Armstrong
Chester W. Nimitz	William
George Marshall	Catlett

PUZ# 23 - ANSWERS
CHRYPTOGRAMS – WWI , KOREA QUOTES

RETREAT? HELL, WE JUST GOT HERE!

Marine Capt. Lloyd Williams – Belleau Wood - WWI

NO GUTS NO GLORY

Major General Frederick C. Blesse - KOREA

FIX BAYONETS! CHARGE! EVERYBODY GOES WITH ME!

Captain Lewis Millett - KOREA

PUZ# 24 - ANSWERS

WWII FACTS – WESTERN EUROPE

April – November 1941 - Western Desert Campaign – Siege of **Tobruk**
July 1942 - Western Desert Campaign – Battle of El **Alamein**
July 1940 - Italian Invasion of **Sudan**
Feb. 1943 – Tunisia - 1st Major US -Axis battle – Battle of **Kasserine** Pass.

23 March 1943 - Tunisia – First US Victory over Axis - Battle of El **Guettar**
23 March – Tunisia – US Commander at El Guetter Pass -**Patton**
23 March – Unit critical to operations in El Guetter – 1st **Ranger** Battalion
June 1940 – December 1942 – Siege of the Island of **Malta**
April 1941 – German invasion of **Greece**
July – August 1943 – Battle of **Sicily**
September 1943 – Operation Slapstick – Invasion of **Italy**
December 1943 – Easter Coast of Italy - Battle of **Ortona**
December 1943 – Bernhardt Line – Monte La Difensa - **Devil's** Brigade
January thru May 1944 – West Coast of Italy – Battle of Monte **Cassino**
January 22, 1944 – Allied Amphibious Landing – Battle of **Anzio**
September 13-24, 1944 – Greek/Canadian/New Zealanders – Battle of **Rimini**
April -June 1940, Europe – Axis Invasion of **Norway**
May 1940 – Europe – Axis Invasion of Belgium, Netherlands and **Luxembourg**
26 May – June 4, 1940 – evacuation of **Dunkerque**
July – October 1940 – In the Air – Battle of **Britain**
June 6, 1944 – Return to Continental Europe – Operation **Overlord**
June 6, 1944 – Normandy Invasion Commander - **Eisenhower**
August 25, 1944 - **Liberation** of Paris
17-25 September, 1944 – Operation **Market** Garden
December 1944 to January 1945 – Easter Belgium – Battle of the **Bulge**
March 24 1945 – U.S. XVIII Airborne / British 6th Airborne cross the **Rhine**

PUZ# 25 - ANSWERS

WWII Battles

PUZ# 26 ANSWER

AIR COMBAT
Where will they meet?

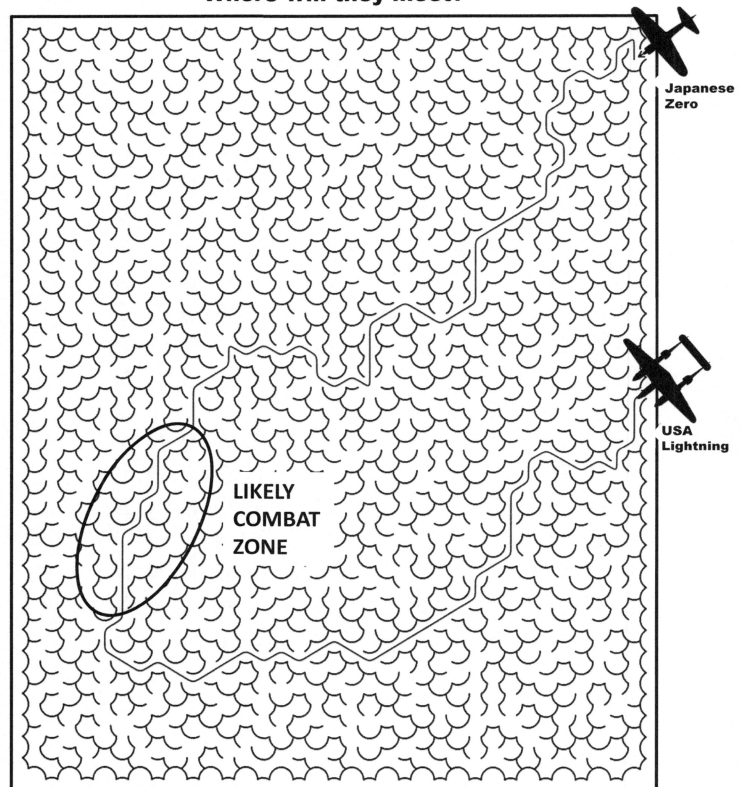

PUZ# 27 - ANSWERS
QUOTES BY GENERALS

THE MILITARY DON'T START WARS. POLITICIANS START WARS.

General William C. Westmoreland

PERPETUAL OPTIMISM IS A FORCE MULTIPLIER

General Colin Powell

IT DOESN'T TAKE A HERO TO ORDER MEN INTO BATTLE. IT TAKES A HERO TO BE ONE OF THOSE MEN WHO GOES INTO BATTLE

General H. Norman Schwarzkopf

PUZ# 28
FRIEND or FOE
ANSWERS

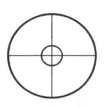

PUZ# 29 – WWII - - OCEAN WAR – ANSWERS

1939 – 1945 Battle of the **Atlantic**

September 1939 – Battle of the River **Plate**

February 16 1940 – HMS Cossack frees prisoners from the German tanker **Altmark**

24 May 1941 – HMS Hood sunk and HMS Prince of Wales damaged by Bismarck and Prinz **Eugen**

July 1942 Convoy PQ 17 lost 24 of 35 ships while heading for the Russian Port of **Arkangelsk**

Cruisers HMS Sheffield and Jamaica vs Cruisers Lutzow and Hipper - Battle of the **Barents** Sea

December 1943 – RN with HMS Duke of York sinks Battleship Scharnhorst. Battle of North **Cape**

1 American Battleship at the landing at Casablanca – USS **Massachusetts**

Aircraft carriers at Casablanca landing – Suwannee and **Ranger**

300nmi west of Brest France - **Bismarck** sunk.

Torpedo Alley off the coast of North **Carolina**

5 May 1945 - Last US flagged ship sunk during the war. SS **Black** Point.

6 May 1945 -USS Ericsson, Amick, Atherton & Moberly; Blimps K-16 & K-58 sink U-853 off Pt. **Judith**

December 7, 1941 **Pearl** Harbor.

December 1941- Battles of Wake and **Guam**

June 1942 – Japanese occupation of **Kiska**

January – April 1942 – Japanese invasion of The **Philippines**

MacArthur consolidated his Philippine forces at Bataan and the island of **Corregidor**

Straight where HMAS Perth and USS Houston were sunk. **Sunda**

Port in Territory of New Guinea – Battle of **Rabaul**

May 1942 – Battle of the Coral **Sea**

June 1942 – Battle of **Midway.** Hint -Neither Here nor There

AKA; Battle of Solomon Sea, Battle of Friday the 13th, Battle of **Guadalcanal**

Aug 6,7 1943 – Destroyers vs Destroyers – Battle of **Vella** Gulf

September – November 1944 – Operation Stalemate – Marines' most bitter battle*. **Peleliu**

October – December 1944 – MacArthur returns – Battle of **Leyte**

Five Weeks in February and March 1945 – Joe Rosenthal's famous picture. **Iwo Jima**

* National Museum of Marines (Archives)

PUZ# 30 - ANSWERS

- CHRYPTOGRAMS –
REVOLUTION AND CIVIL WAR

IF THEY MEAN TO HAVE A WAR, LET IT START HERE!

Captain John Parker Lexington April 19, 1775

WAR IS HELL

General William Tecumseh Sherman

THERE IS JACKSON STANDING LIKE A STONE WALL

Brigadier General Barnard Elliot Bee – At Bull Run

TRIVIA

PUZ #1 - ACES - TRIVIA

ACES

GERMANY
Eric Hartmann – 352 victories – Top Ace of all time – Double ace in one day
Erich Rudorffer – 222 victories – Double jet ace in a day (Me262)

FINLAND
Hans Wind – 75 victories - Finnish Ace – Five times ace in a day
Eino Luukkanen – 56 victories

GREAT BRITAIN
Robert Stanford Tuck – 30 victories
Nevil Duke - 27 victories

UNITED STATES of AMERICA
Gregory Boyington – 28 victories - 6 with AVG and 22 with USMC
David McCampbell – 34 victories – Top US Navy Ace
Richard I. Bong – 40 victories – Top US Ace

USSR
Ivan Koshedub – 66 victories – Highest Scoring Allied Ace
Aleksandr Pokryshkin – 59 victories

JAPAN
Shigeo Fukumoto – 72 victories
Shoichi Sugita – 70 victories

NOT ACES -
Hosato Takei – American - Better known as George Takei or Mr. Sulu
David Diehl – American - Football player for the New York Giants – Super Bowl XLVI winner
Yari Kurri – Finnish - Right Winger - 5 time Stanley Cup champion – Hall of Famer
Spencer Chaplin – Englishman - Charles Spencer Chaplin KBE, Better known as 'Charlie Chaplin'
Michael Faraday – Englishman - Scientist – electromagnetism, 'Faraday's Law of Induction'
Roger Sherman – American – Member - Committee of Five - drafted the Declaration of Independence
Roy Harold Scherer – American – Better known as Rock Hudson - Actor
Yully Borisovich – Russian born American - Better known as Yul Brynner – Actor

PUZ#1 - MORE ACES TRIVIA

THE 25 TOP U.S. Flying Aces

Richard I Bong -	US Army Air Force	40 Victories	Top U.S. Ace	✝
Thomas B. McGuire	US Army Air Force	38 Victories		✝
David McCampbell	US Navy	34 Victories	Two times Ace in a Day	
Francis 'Gabby' Gabreski	US Army Air Force	28 Victories	6 in Korean War	
Gregory 'Pappy' Boyington	AVG / USMC	28 Victories	6 AVG / 22 USMC	
Robert S. Johnson	US Army Air Force	27 Victories		
Charles H. MacDonald	US Army Air Force	27 Victories		
George E. Preddy Jr.	US Army Air Force	27 Victories	Ace in a Day	✝
Joseph J. Foss	US Marine Corps	26 Victories	Top Ace for USMC only	
Robert M. Hanson	US Marine Corps	25 Victories		✝
John C. Meyer	US Army Air Force	24 Victories	2 in Korea	
Cecil E. Harris	US Navy	24 Victories		
Eugene A Valencia	US Navy	23 Victories		
Lance C. Wade	Royal Air Force	23 Victories		✝
David C. Schilling	US Army Air Force	22 Victories		
Gerald R. Johnson	US Army Air Force	22 Victories		
Neel E. Kearby	US Army Air Force	22 Victories		✝
Jay T. Robbins	US Army Air Force	22 Victories		
Dominic S. Gentile	US Army Air Force	22 Victories	2 with the RAF	
Fred J. Christensen	US Army Air Force	21 Victories		
Raymond S. Wetmore	US Army Air Force	21 Victories		
John J. Voll	US Army Air Force	21 Victories		
Kenneth A. Walsh	US Marine Corps	21 Victories		
Walker 'Bud' Melville Mahurin	US Army Air Force	21 Victories	3 in Korea	
Donald N. Aldrich	US Marine Corps	20 Victories		

WWII USN BATTLESHIPS

Wyoming Class – (1912 – 1947)

    Wyoming – Arkansas

    12 X 12" guns in 6 two gun turrets

New York Class – (1914 – 1946)

    New York – Texas

    10 X 14" guns in 5 two gun turrets

Nevada Class – (1916 – 1946)

    Nevada[1] – Oklahoma[3]

    10 X 14" (2 X 2gun turrets and 2 x 3 gun turrets)

    First US – Standard Type Battleships

Pennsylvania Class – (1916 – 1946)

    Pennsylvania[1] – Arizona[3]

    12 X 14" in 4 turrets

New Mexico Class - (1917 – 1956)

    New Mexico – Mississippi – Idaho

    12 X 14" in 3 turrets

Tennessee Class – (1920 – 1947)

    Tennessee[1] – California[2]

    12 X 14" guns in 3 turrets

Colorado Class – (1921 -1947)

    Colorado – Maryland[1] – West Virginia[2]

    8 X 16" guns in 4 turret

North Carolina Class – (1941 – 1947)

    North Carolina – Washington

    9 X 16" guns in 3 turrets

South Dakota Class (1942 – 1947)

    South Dakota – Indiana – Massachusetts – Alabama

    9 X 16" guns in 3 turrets

Iowa Class – (1943-1958 – 1968-1969 – 1982-1992)

    Iowa – New Jersey – Missouri - Wisconsin9 X 16" guns in 3 turrets

    Only Battleships with Tomahawk and Harpoon Missiles

1. Damaged at Pearl Harbor
2. Sunk at Pearl Harbor – Refloated
3. Sunk at Pearl Harbor

PUZ#3 - TRIVIA

PUZ #5 - TRIVIA

INTERESTING FACTS FROM THE NAME QUIZ

1. Brigadier General – US Air Force – Paul Tibbets – Pilot of Enola Gay
2. Vice Admiral – Netherlands Navy – Conrad Helfrich – Commander ABDA Naval Force – 1942 (American-British-Dutch-Australian)
3. Rear Admiral – Netherlands Navy - Karel Doorman – Died in the Battle of the Java Sea
4. Lieutenant General – Canadian Army – Andrew McNaughton – First President of the UN Security Council
5. Sergeant – US Army – Bill Mauldin – Creator of "Willie and Joe" Stars and Stripes cartoon soldiers
6. General – Japanese Army – Hideki Tojo – Executed for war crimes -1948
7. Fleet Admiral – Japanese Navy – Isoroku Yamamoto – His plane was shot down in 1943 by US fighters
8. Air Chief Marshal – Royal Air Force – Hugh Dowding – Commander at Battle of Britain
9. General de Brigade – Army of France – Charles de Gaulle – Future President of France
10. General of the Army – US Army – Dwight D. Eisenhower – Future President of the United States
11. General of the Army – US Army – Douglas MacArthur – Rebuilt Japan after the war
12. General – US Army – George Patton – Died in a road accident 4 months after the end of the war in Europe

PUZ #7 - TRIVIA

Andrew Jackson's 1862 Valley Campaign
Timeline

Point	Event
1	January 23-30, 1862 - Jackson's Army return to Winchester
	March 11, 1862 - Thomas J. Jackson evacuates Winchester
8	March 18, 1862 - Skirmish at Middletown
10	March 23, 1862 - First Battle of Kernstown, south of Winchester
	March 24, 1862 - Jackson's army retreats
20	April 17, 1862 - Federals reach Mount Jackson and New Market
23	April 22, 1862 - Union troops occupy Harrisonburg
26	April 30, 1862 - Jackson sets out towards Staunton
43	May 8, 1862 - Battle of McDowell
52	May 21 Return to New Market
62	May 23, 1862 - Battle of Front Royal – **Jackson Victory**
65	May 25, 1862 – Battle of Winchester - **Jackson Victory**
69	May 26, 1862 - Jackson moves toward Harpers Ferry
	. Jackson is forced to retreat
85	June 6, 1862 – Battle of Harrisonburg - **Jackson Victory**
89	June 8, 1862 - Battle of Cross Keys - **Jackson Victory**
90	June 9, 1862 - Battle of Port Republic - **Jackson Victory**
95	June 17, 1862 - Jackson leaves the Valley headed for Richmond.

PUZ# 8 – TRIVIA
FAMOUS U.S. BATTLES - Timeline

- Battle of Lexington and Concord – April 1775
- Battle of Fort Ticonderoga – May 1775
- Battle of Bunker Hill – June 1775
- Battle of Saratoga – Sept – Oct 1777
- Battle of the Alamo – Feb 23-Mar 6 1836
- Battle of Fort Sumter – April 1861
- Siege of Yorktown – April – May 1862
- Battle of Antietam – Sept 1862
- Gettysburg – July 1863
- Battle of the Little Big Horn – June 1876
- Battle of San Juan Hill – July 1898
- Pearl Harbor – December 1941
- Battle of the Coral Sea - May 1942
- Battle of Midway - June 1942
- Battle of Guadalcanal – Aug 1942 – Feb 1943
- Battle of Monte Cassino Jan – May 1944
- Battle of Anzio – Jan – June 1944
- Battle of the Philippine Sea - June 1944
- Battle of Leyte Gulf – Oct 1944
- D-Day - June 1944
- Battle of the Bulge - Dec – Jan 1945
- Battle of Luzon – Jan – Aug 1945
- Battle of Iwo Jima Feb-Mar 1945
- Battle of Okinawa – April 1- June 22 1945
- Battle of the Pusan Perimeter – Aug – Sept 1950
- Battle of Inchon – Sept '50
- The Tet Offensive – Jan '68
- Battle of Khe Sanh – Jan – July '68
- Iraq War – March 2003
- Battle of Baghdad – April 2003
- Battle of Basra - March 2008

TRIVIA

PUZ# 9   NORMANDY INVASION - TRIVIA

- Normandy Invasion – code name – Operation Overlord
- Planning for Overlord started in 1943
- Over 3,200 reconnaissance missions were conducted in preparation
- There were five landing zones AMERICAN (Utah and Omaha) BRITISH (Gold and Sword) and CANADIAN (Juno)
- The 'D' stood for DAY – That is June 6 – Day-Day.
- A phantom army was built to deceive the Germans – Under General G. Patton. The Germans were convinced that Patton would lead any invasion by the allies.
- Garbo – was a Spanish double agent who fed the Germans misinformation
- Germany had used 100,000 workers to build the 'Atlantic Wall' fortifications
- Swimming tanks, flame throwing tanks and collapsible motorcycles were among the new inventions created for the invasion
- 30 Women of the 'Women's Auxiliary Air Force' were sent to local pubs to see if troops would talk about secret plans – (None Did)
- Eisenhower quote from the eve of the invasion "The eyes of the world are upon you." – He also pre-wrote a message for potential failure accepting all blame.
- Of the 6,939 vessels involved, 4,126 were landing craft.
- The naval forces assembled at a point in the English Channel off the Isle of Wight called 'Piccadilly Circus.'
- Not the largest 'Single Day' invasion of all time. Overlord (156,000 troops) – Operation 'HUSKY' the Sicily invasion (160,000 troops)
- Code to alert French Resistance included "the dice is on the carpet"
- 7.000.000 pounds of bombs were dropped on D-Day. 10,521 combat aircraft flew 15,000 sorties. 113 aircraft were lost. For troop transport 2,000 aircraft and 867 gliders were used. 1,900 bombers preceded the invasion with an attack at 3am.
- The flat bottom 'Higgins Boat' was originally designed for the shallow waters of the Mississippi and gulf shores. The original Design was called the 'Eureka Boat'
- Heaviest losses were by the BRITISH (17,769), AMERICAN (9,386) CANADIAN (5,002) – GERMANS (77,866)
- Actor Richard Todd (Major John Howard – The Longest Day) actually fought in the real landing – He was an officer in the 7th Para.
- Actor James Doohan (Scotty – Star Trek) fought at D-Day in the Royal Canadian Artillery.

PUZ# 10 — Presidential Military Service Interesting Facts

PRESIDENT (General ★)	SERVED Y/N	ARMY	NAVY	AIR FORCE	NOTES - AWARDS
Washington ★★★★★	Y	X			French & Indian War/American Revolution General of the Army
Adams	N				
Jefferson	Y	X			American Revolution
Madison	Y	X			American Revolution
Monroe	Y	X			American Revolution
J. Quincy Adams	N				
Andrew Jackson ★★	Y	X			American Revolution/War of 1812/Creek War/ 1st Seminole War
Van Buren	N				
W.H. Harrison	Y	X			N.W. Indian War / War of 1812
Tyler	Y	X			War 1812
Polk	Y	X			Militia
Zachary Taylor ★★	Y	X			War of 1812 / Black Hawk War/ 2nd Seminole War / Mexican-American War
Fillmore	Y	X			Civil War - Militia
Pierce ★	Y	X			Mexican-American War
Buchanan	Y	X			War of 1812
Lincoln	Y	X			Black Hawk War
Andrew Johnson ★	Y	X			Civil War
Grant ★★★★★	Y	X			Civil War – General of the Army
Hayes ★★	Y	X			Civil War
Garfield ★★	Y	X			Civil War
Arthur ★	Y	X			Civil War JAG corps
Cleveland	N				Paid $150 dollars for a replacement to the Civil war
B. Harrison ★	Y	X			Civil War
McKinley	Y	X			Civil War
Teddy Roosevelt	Y	X			Spanish American War - Medal of Honor
Taft	Y	X			Home Guard WWI/Secretary of War 1904-08
Wilson	N				
Harding	N				
Coolidge	N				
Hoover	N				
F.D. Roosevelt	N				Ass't Secretary of the Navy
Truman	Y	X			WWI - France
Eisenhower ★★★★★	Y	X			Supreme Allied Commander - Europe
Kennedy	Y		X		Navy & Marine Corp Metal – Purple Heart
Lyndon Johnson	Y		X		Silver Star
Nixon	Y		X		2 Battle Stars
Ford	Y		X		WWII
Carter	Y		X		Sea Duty - Korea
Reagan	Y			X	Stateside Service
George H.W. Bush	Y		X		WWII - DFC
Clinton	N				
George W. Bush	Y			X	Stateside Service
Barack Obama	N				
Donald Trump	N				

TRIVIA

Famous Planes and Pilots – Interesting Facts

PUZ# 14 - TRIVIA

Jimmy Stewart (actor) (2- Distinguished Flying Crosses, Air Medal with three Oak Leaf Clusters and the French Croix de Guerre). He flew B-24 Liberators as part of the 703 Bombardment Squadron, 445 and 453 Bombardment Groups, After the war as a reservist Stewart rose to the rank of Brigadier General and flew Convair B-36 Peacemakers, B-47 Stratojets and B-52 Stratofortresses including one mission as an observer in Vietnam.

Jimmy Doolittle – General – (Medal of Honor, DSM (Army), Silver Star, DFC, Bronze Star, Air Medal, Presidential medal of Freedom) – Winner - Schneider Trophy, Bendix Trophy, Thompson Trophy and Harmon Trophy, test pilot, first pilot to perform an outside loop (previously thought to be a fatal maneuver), set a wold high speed record of 296 miles per hour in 1932. Then planned and led a top-secret attack on the Japanese Homeland in April 1942. The Doolittle Raid of 16 B-25 bombers made a one-way bombing raid, taking off from the U.S. Aircraft Carrier Hornet. After successfully making their attack, Doolittle's plane ran out of fuel and the crew bailed out over China. After returning to the U.S. Doolittle continued to serve in North Africa receiving 4 Air Medals.

Greg Boyington – Colonel – (Medal of Honor, Navy Cross, Purple Heart) Resigned a commission in the USMC to join and become a flight leader with the legendary AVG 'Flying Tigers' in China. In 1942 Boyington returned to the USMC and eventually became the Commanding Officer of Marine Fighter Squadron 214, better known as the "Black Sheep'. Boyington was shot down over Rabaul on his 48th mission after downing his 26th enemy plane. He survived 20 months in a Japanese POW camp and was liberated after the bombings of Hiroshima and Nagasaki.

Richard Bong – Major – (Medal of Honor, DSC, Silver Star, DFC, Air medal) Bong was reprimanded "For looping the Golden gate bridge, flying at a low level down Market Street in San Francisco, and blowing the clothes off of an Oakland lady's clothesline." He was told by General Kenny, commanding Officer of 4th Air Force, "If you didn't want to fly down Market Street I wouldn't want you in my Air Force. But you are not to do it any more." Bong became the highest-scoring flying ace in the U.S. with 40 victories.

Charles Older – Flying Ace with the AVG in China, and with the Army Air Force in Burma. Older flew B-26 Invader aircraft in Korea and is also famous for being the Judge in the Charles Manson trail.

Paul Warfield Tibbets – Bomber Pilot – (DFC, DSC, Air Medal, Legion of Merit and Purple Heart) – Flew the lead plane in the first American 100 plane, daylight bombing and 43 bombing missions over Europe, and was the pilot of the 'Enola Gay' (Named after his mother) – for the bombing of Hiroshima and Nagasaki.

Famous Planes and Pilots – Interesting Facts

PUZ# 14 - TRIVIA

Hap Arnold – General – (DSM (Army), Legion of Merit, DFC, Air Medal) – Only US Air Force officer to hold 5-Star rank, Only officer to hold 5-Star rank in two different services. Tought to fly by the Wright Brothers he was one of the first military pilots worldwide. He was a silent film stunt pilot (where re received his nickname "Happy" latter shortened to 'Hap'). Supported Billy Mitchell, testifying at his court-martial and after-words continued the work of support for air-power and creation of the U.S. Air Force.

Clair Chennault – Lt-General – (DSM (Army) (2), DFC (2), Order of the Cloud and Banner, Order of the British Empire (Commander), Order of the Blue Sky and White Sun) – America's first military leader of the Second World War. Led the 'Three Musketeers" aerobatic Team in 1928-1932, Resigned from the US forces in 1937 due to poor health. Became Chiang-Kai-shek's chief air advisor in August 1937. He personally flew scouting missions against Japanese forces in a Curtiss H-75 fighter. Returned to the US to enlist for and create the AVG (American Volunteer Group) – "The Flying Tigers". Returned to the Air Force in 1942 as a Colonel and soon became a Brigadier-General the major-general of the 14th Air Force in China. After the war Chennault created a anti-communist Civil Air Transport organization later called "Air America" which did work in Indochina, Burma, and Vietnam.

Roy Marlin 'Butch' Voris – WWII Flying Ace, (DFC, Air Medal)– Assembled and Trained the first "Blue Angels" demonstration Team then known simply as the "Navy Flight Exhibition Team" with Sea Blue and Gold F6F-5 Hellcats and then F8F-1 Bearcats. The name "Blue Angels' came from a nightclub in New York.

Captain Christopher Magee – Fighter Ace USMC – (Navy Cross) 'Black Sheep' Squadron. After the war he fought with the Israeli Haganah, flying the Avia S-199 – A Czechoslovakian version of the Messerschmitt Bf 109. He returned to the US and became a bank robber and served 6 years in prison. Magee's brother John Gillespie Magee Jr. was a pilot, author and poet famous for his poem, 'High Flight'

Bob Hoover – Pilot - (DFC, Soldier's medal of Valor, Air Medal w/clusters, Croix de Guerre, Purple Heart) – Shot down over Sicily, captured, escaped from a prisoner of war camp, stole a Fw-190 and flew to Holland. Chuck Yeager's backup pilot on the Bell X-1 program – Hoover is most famous for his Air Show performances in his P-51 Mustang 'Ole Yeller' and Aero Shrike Commander. Hoover could successfully pour a cup of tea while performing a 1G barrel roll. Hoover's Shrike Commander can be found in the Smithsonian Air and Space Museum.

Famous Planes and Pilots – Interesting Facts

PUZ# 14 - TRIVIA

Alexander Jefferson – Fighter pilot and prisoner of war (Congressional Gold Medal, DFC. Air Medal and Purple Heart (presented 57 years late) – member of the famous Tuskegee Airmen and Author of the book 'Red Tail'.

Nancy Harkness Love – Pilot (Air Medal) - Founder and commander of the 'Women's Auxiliary Ferry Squadron' and latter the 'Women Air Force Service Pilots' (WASP). Qualified over 300 women pilots on advanced military aircraft.

Ola Rexroat – Pilot – (Congressional Gold Medal) – Had the dangerous job of flying planes towing targets for ground artillery before joining the Women Airforce Service Pilots and then the US Air Force – After the war she was a career Air Traffic Controller. Ola was the only Native American Woman to serve in the WASPs.

Edward 'Butch' O'Hare – Lt-Commander U.S. Navy – (Medal of Honor, Navy Cross, DFC, Purple Heart) – On February 20, 1942, Lt O'Hare and his wingman were the only fighters in the air when a second wave of Japanese bombers attacked the Carrier Lexington. With his wingman's guns jammed, O'Hare shot down three bombers single handed and damaged two. His attack affected the bombers attack and none of their bombs struck the Lexington. His effort won Lt. O'Hare the Medal of Honor. Another interesting fact – O'Hare's father, a lawyer in Chicago, was shot and killed probably by Al Capone's gang after helping to convict Capone's of tax evasion. O'Hare's Wildcat can be found at the west end of Terminal 2 at O'Hare International Airport, Chicago.

George H.W. Bush – Lieutenant – (DFC, Air Medal, Presidential Citation) - Flew 58 combat missions. He was shot down by anti-aircraft fire over Chichi-jima, an island about 600 miles south of Japan. He managed to get clear of the island and bail out over the Pacific. Bush went into business after the war and after graduating from Harvard and later had a reasonably successful political career :) – Congressman, Ambassador to U.N., Envoy to China, Director of the CIA, Vice President and President of the United States

PUZ# 15   TANK TRIVIA

- Prior to WWII German tanks were actually inferior to the tanks of allied armies however their tanks tactics (Blitzkrieg) proved far superior. An important addition to German tanks was radios which provided command and control and flexible application of firepower.
- As WWII progressed tanks evolved from 'Light Tanks' which generally disappeared by the end of the war while 'Medium Tanks' grew from 20 tons to 30 to 45 tons.
- Turrets which were originally thought to be interesting but not essential became standard.
- Older and lighter tank chassis were used for Self –Propelled guns with fixed casements – Soviet T34 had an 85mm gun in its turret but a 100mm gun when converted to a fixed casement. The German 'Panzer I 'Light Tanks' were modified to carry fixed 47mm anti-tank guns.
- The Soviets ended the war with more tanks than the rest of the world combined - 18,000 – 22,000.
- British tank doctrine covered 'Infantry Tanks' - Slow, heavily armoured – designed to crawl along with foot soldiers, and 'Cruiser Tanks' - Fast at the cost of armour - – designed for fast breakout and flanking maneuvers.
- Even after Pearl Harbor the 10th Armoured Division of the US Army had NO tanks
- US Tanks – M3 – 'Stuart' (Light Tank), M3 'Lee' and 'Grant' (Medium Tank) were the best tanks available to the Allies early in the war. M4 'Sherman' 1942 – Equal to German medium tanks. The M4 was used by all Allied forces and was the second most produced tank of the war with 40,000 produced.

PUZ# 15   TANK TRIVIA

- Japan fielded mostly older designs (Type 95 Ha-Go, Type 97 Chi-Ha) in the Pacific which were no match for more modern Allied tanks.
- Later Japanese Tanks Type 3 Chi-Nu were restricted in production due to lack of materials
- Type 2 Ho-I (Infantry Support), Type 1 Ho-Ni (Tank Destroyer) were produced in limited numbers.
- Italian tanks included mostly tankettes armed only with machine guns.
- The Fiat M11/39 was fielded in 1940 with a 37mm gun followed by the M13/40, M14/41 and M15/42 all with 47mm guns. All were light tanks.
- A heavier P40 with a 75mm gun never saw service

PUZ# 19 – GUADALCANAL - TRIVIA

13 November 1942 – off Guadalcanal

A Japanese force under Admiral Hiroaki Abe, started its journey down the 'SLOT' into New Georgia Sound into Savo Sound (soon to be known as Ironbottom Sound. In addition to the two battleships *Hiei* (Abe's flagship) and *Kirishima*, Abe's force included the light cruiser *Nagara* and 11 destroyers Three more destroyers would provide a rear guard.

US forces had spotted the Japanese ships and Admiral Daniel J Callaghan was ordered to intercept. Callaghan prepared his force to meet the Japanese that night in the sound. His force consisted of two heavy cruisers(*San Francisco* and *Portland*), three light cruisers (*Helena*, *Juneau*, and *Atlanta*), and eight destroyers: *Cushing*, *Laffey*, *Sterett*, *O'Bannon*, *Aaron Ward*, *Barton*, *Monssen*, and *Fletcher*. Admiral Callaghan commanded from *San Francisco*.

At about 01:25 on 13 November, in near-complete darkness due to the bad weather and dark moon, the ships of the Imperial Japanese force entered the sound. Unlike their American counterparts, the Japanese had trained extensively in night battle. This experience would be critical.

Several of the U.S. ships detected the approaching Japanese on radar, beginning at 01:24, but had trouble communicating the information to Callaghan. Messages were sent and received but did not reach the commander who was not commanding from a radar equipped ship but rather commanded from the bridge of San Francisco with a limited picture of the situation.

Several minutes after initial radar contact the two forces sighted each other, at about the same time, but both Abe and Callaghan for different and various reasons hesitated ordering their ships into action.

At 01:48, *Akatsuki* and *Hiei* turned on large searchlights and illuminated *Atlanta* only 3,000 yds away. Several ships on both sides spontaneously began firing, and the formations of the two adversaries quickly disintegrated. Callaghan realized his ships were nearly surrounded by Japanese ships and gave an order - 'Odd ships fire to starboard, even ships fire to port' yet no pre-battle order had designated ships by odd or even. A general melee described as a barroom brawl ensued. Most US ships initially fired at the destroyer Akatsuki since she had her search lights on. Most Japanese ships turned on Atlanta, the lead cruiser. Somewhere in the early moments of the battle San Francisco mistakenly fired on Atlanta doing considerable damage. Soon US fire turned on Hiele with her huge size and nine searchlights. The destroyers Laffey, Sterett and O'Bannon all attacked the battleship doing considerable damage. Laffey raked Hiele's bridge wounding Abe and killing his chief of staff.

Hiele concentrated on San Francisco.

San Francisco was hit by shells from Hiele, Kirishima, Inazuma and Ikazuchi killing Admiral Callaghan, Captain Cassin Young and most of the bridge staff.

RESULT
American Ships:
Portland - heavily damaged
San Francisco – heavily damaged
Cushing – sunk
Laffey – sunk
Barton – sunk
Juneau – heavily damaged
Monssen – sunk
Sterett – heavily damaged
Aron Ward –

Japanese Ships:
Akatsuki – sunk
Amatsukaze – heavily damaged
Yudachi – sunk

Battleship Hiele 1942

PUZ#19 - GUADALCANAL TRIVIA

Hiroaki Abe was an admiral in the Imperial Japanese Navy during World War II. During the Naval Battle of Guadalcanal on 12–13 November, when assigned to bombard Henderson Field on Guadalcanal, he broke off his attack after encountering U.S. Navy Rear Admiral Daniel Callaghan's Task Group 67.4 (TG 67.4). Abe lost his flagship, the battleship *Hiei*, which he ordered scuttled after it had been seriously damaged, as well as two destroyers. Abe himself was wounded - and his Chief-of-Staff (Captain Masakane Suzuki) was killed - by machine-gun fire from the USS *Laffey* (DD-459), a destroyer that he sank afterwards. His failure to aggressively push through his attack against what appeared to be an inferior enemy force created tremendous controversy, and he was relieved of his command by Admiral Isoroku Yamamoto.

USS San Francisco

Daniel J. Callaghan - During the Guadalcanal Campaign on November 13, 1942, he was on the bridge of the USS *San Francisco* when incoming enemy fire killed him and most of his command staff He received the Medal of Honor posthumously for his efforts in this battle.

Following the explosion, Lieutenant Commander Bruce McCandless assumed operational command of the *San Francisco* and despite the deaths of so many senior officers, the battle ended in a strategic victory for the Allied side. Analysis of the battle led to a rapid improvement in USN techniques for fighting in poor visibility, particularly in the adoption of combat information centers.

Callaghan's brother Vice-Admiral - William Callaghan would later become the first captain of the USS *Missouri* (BB-63).

PUZ#21 - TRIVIA   MARINE WORDS
Meanings

ALICE – All-Purpose Light Individual Carry Equipment
ALPHAS – Service Alpha Uniform
ARMY – Ain't Ready to be a Marine Yet
VMFA – Marine Fighter Attack Squadron
BarneyStyle – Understandable to idiots
Blooper – Thump-Gun, Grenade Launcher
Boot – Fresh out of Boot Camp
Bulkhead – Wall
CanoeU – Annapolis Naval Academy – Also 'South Maryland Small Boat and Barge Institute'
CASEVAC – Casualty Evacuation
CONUS – CONtinental United States – Also – 'Land of the Big PX'
Cumshaw – Given as a favour or gift – 'Kamsia' Chinese for 'grateful thanks'
Deck – Floor
Disneyland – Marine Corps Headquarters
Gangway – Ship passageway – Also – Get out of the way!
Geedunk – Candy or where to find it
Homeslice – Civilian (homeboy)
Jarhead – Not a Marine term – Mistakenly used by uninformed beings from other services.
LCPLIC – Lance Corporal In-Charge
Leatherneck – Marine
Gunny – Gunnery Sergeant
MEDEVAC – MEDical EVACuation
NAVY – Never Again Volunteer Yourself
Schmuckatelli – unnamed (less than competent) junior marine
SemperFi – Semper Fidelis 'Always Faithful'
Oorah – Means Oo Rah. Actually can mean a lot of things. If you are a Marine you get it.

PUZ# 22 - TRIVIA

US Generals with their Middle names or Nicknames
Interesting facts

Ulysses S. 'Simpson' Grant - Simpson was not part of his name at all and that's on the authority of the man himself. On June 23, 1864, Grant wrote to Congressman E.B. Washburn with an explanation, politely noting, "In answer to your letter of a few days ago asking what stands for in my name I can only state nothing." Yes, it's largely inconsequential minutia, and one wonders why a congressman queried the commander-in-chief of the army over it while civil war ravaged the nation but it's also a reminder that even the simplest historical questions are often not so simple. Grant goes on to explain that the misnomer originated from the congressman who assisted his application to West Point. According to Grant, Senator Morris of Ohio had erroneously named him as "Ulysses S. Grant." While Simpson was Grant's mother's maiden name and the name of his brother, it had never been in his name. In fact, he was baptized *Hiram* Ulysses Grant, though known from the very beginning as "Ulysses."

George Washington - Lord Cornwallis was the person said to be responsible for giving Washington the nickname 'The Old Fox'.

Robert E. Lee - Marse Robert – southern slang for 'Master Robert' .

Winfield Scott - Known as "Old Fuss and Feathers" and the "Grand Old Man of the Army", he served on active duty as a general longer than any other person in American history. Over the course of his 53-year career, he commanded forces in the War of 1812, the Black Hawk War, the Mexican–American War, and the Second Seminole War and was the army's senior officer at the start of the American Civil War. Scott conceived the Union strategy known as the Anaconda Plan to defeat the Confederacy.

Douglas MacArthur - An American five-star general and Field Marshal of the Philippine Army. The Japanese gave him the nickname Gaijin Shogun ("foreign military ruler") but not until around the time of his death in 1964.

TRIVIA **Famous Planes and Pilots – Interesting Facts**

Hap Arnold – General – (DSM (Army), Legion of Merit, DFC, Air Medal) – Only US Air Force officer to hold 5-Star rank, Only officer to hold 5-Star rank in two different services. Tought to fly by the Wright Brothers he was one of the first military pilots worldwide. He was a silent film stunt pilot (where re received his nickname "Happy" latter shortened to 'Hap'). Supported Billy Mitchell, testifying at his court-martial and after-words continued the work of support for air-power and creation of the U.S. Air Force.

Clair Chennault – Lt-General – (DSM (Army) (2), DFC (2), Order of the Cloud and Banner, Order of the British Empire (Commander), Order of the Blue Sky and White Sun) – America's first military leader of the Second World War. Led the 'Three Musketeers" aerobatic Team in 1928-1932, Resigned from the US forces in 1937 due to poor health. Became Chiang-Kai-shek's chief air advisor in August 1937. He personally flew scouting missions against Japanese forces in a Curtiss H-75 fighter. Returned to the US to enlist for and create the AVG (American Volunteer Group) – "The Flying Tigers". Returned to the Air Force in 1942 as a Colonel and soon became a Brigadier-General the major-general of the 14th Air Force in China. After the war Chennault created a anti-communist Civil Air Transport organization later called "Air America" which did work in Indochina, Burma, and Vietnam.

Roy Marlin 'Butch' Voris – WWII Flying Ace, (DFC, Air Medal)– Assembled and Trained the first "Blue Angels" demonstration Team then known simply as the "Navy Flight Exhibition Team" with Sea Blue and Gold F6F-5 Hellcats and then F8F-1 Bearcats. The name "Blue Angels' came from a nightclub in New York.

Captain Christopher Magee – Fighter Ace USMC – (Navy Cross) 'Black Sheep' Squadron. After the war he fought with the Israeli Haganah, flying the Avia S-199 – A Czechoslovakian version of the Messerschmitt Bf 109. He returned to the US and became a bank robber and served 6 years in prison. Magee's brother John Gillespie Magee Jr. was a pilot, author and poet famous for his poem, 'High Flight'

Bob Hoover – Pilot - (DFC, Soldier's medal of Valor, Air Medal w/clusters, Croix de Guerre, Purple Heart) – Shot down over Sicily, captured, escaped from a prisoner of war camp, stole a Fw-190 and flew to Holland. Chuck Yeager's backup pilot on the Bell X-1 program – Hoover is most famous for his Air Show performances in his P-51 Mustang 'Ole Yeller' and Aero Shrike Commander. Hoover could successfully pour a cup of tea while performing a 1G barrel roll. Hoover's Shrike Commander can be found in the Smithsonian Air and Space Museum.

PUZ#28 - TRIVIA

Neutral - Greek WWI Cruiser 'Georgio Averof'. The last *armored cruiser* in the world to be commissioned. Italian Built with British guns. She was ceased by the French and eventually returned to Greece after Greece formally entered the war on the side of the allies.

Russian Krivak Class Guided Missile Frigate 'Ladnyy' member of the Russian 'Black Sea' Fleet. She is most famous for the misfire of one of her SS-N-14 missiles during the 2015 Navy Day celebrations in Sevastopol. The missile spiralled out of control and splashed harmlessly into the sea.

PUZ#28 - TRIVIA

'Minsk' - First of 28, Soviet Navy - Ropucha-class Landing Ships.

'USS Bowfin' (SS-287) – A WWII Balao-class submarine – currently moored in Pearl Harbor Hawaii next to the USS Arizona.

'USS Texas' (BB-35) – New York-class dreadnought Battleship – Served in the North Sea in WWI and escorted convoys in WWII. She also provided fire support for Omaha beach on D-Day. She is the only remaining capital ship to have served in both World Wars. She is currently berthed in the San Jacinto Battleground, near Houston

Made in the USA
Las Vegas, NV
21 November 2022

59932731R00057